ROBERT FILLIOU

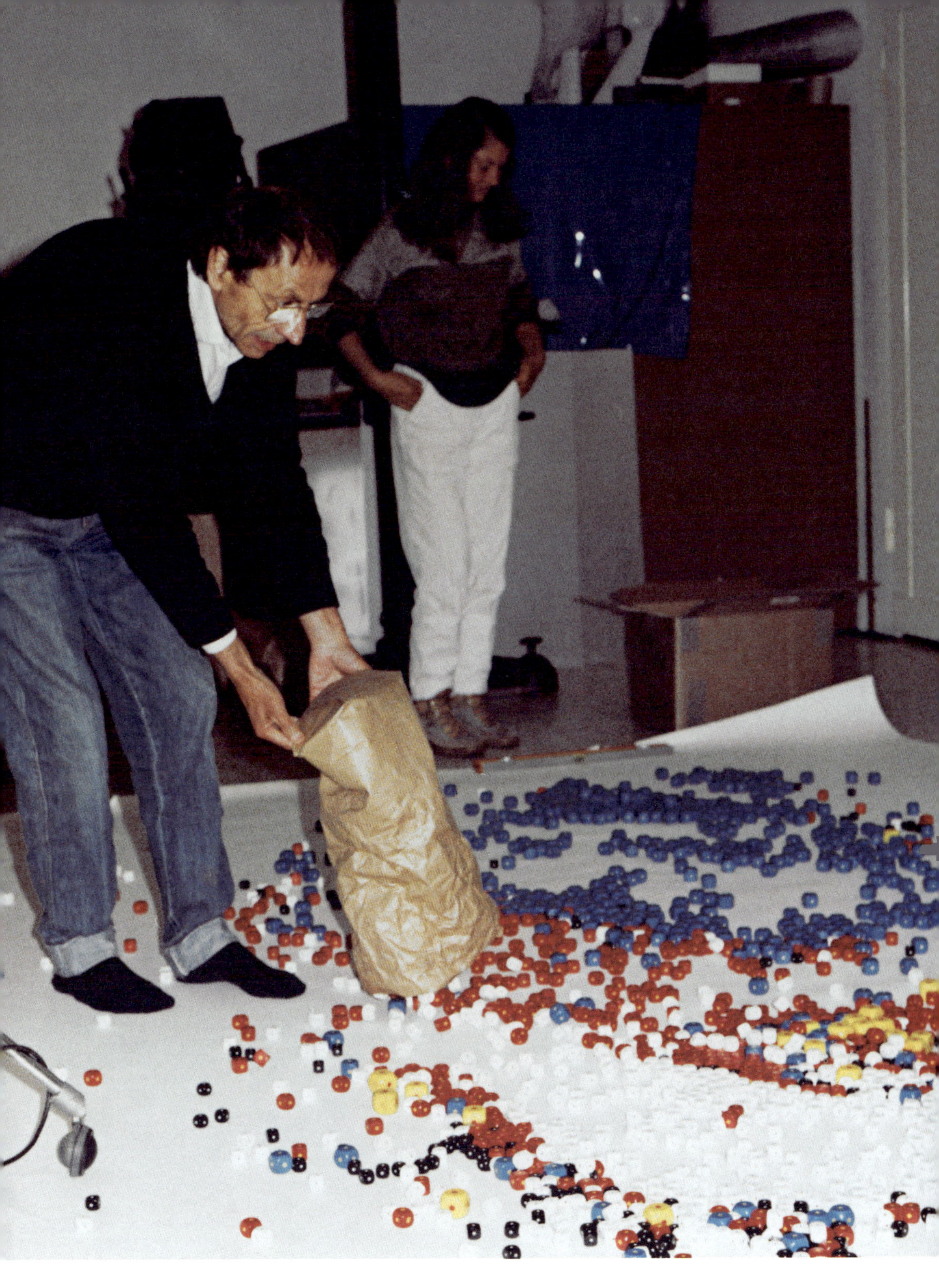

Robert Filliou placing the dices for *EINS. UN. ONE…*

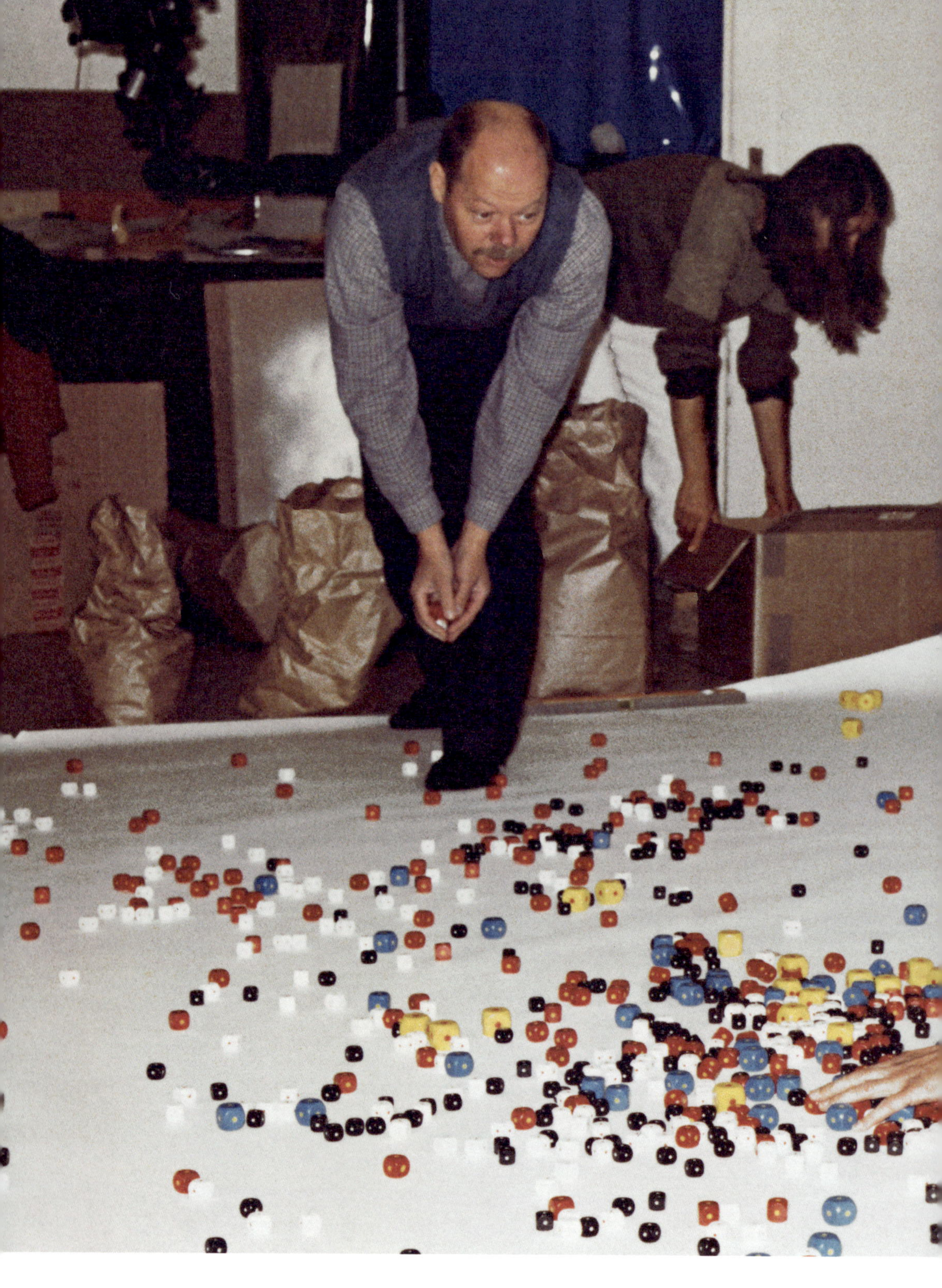

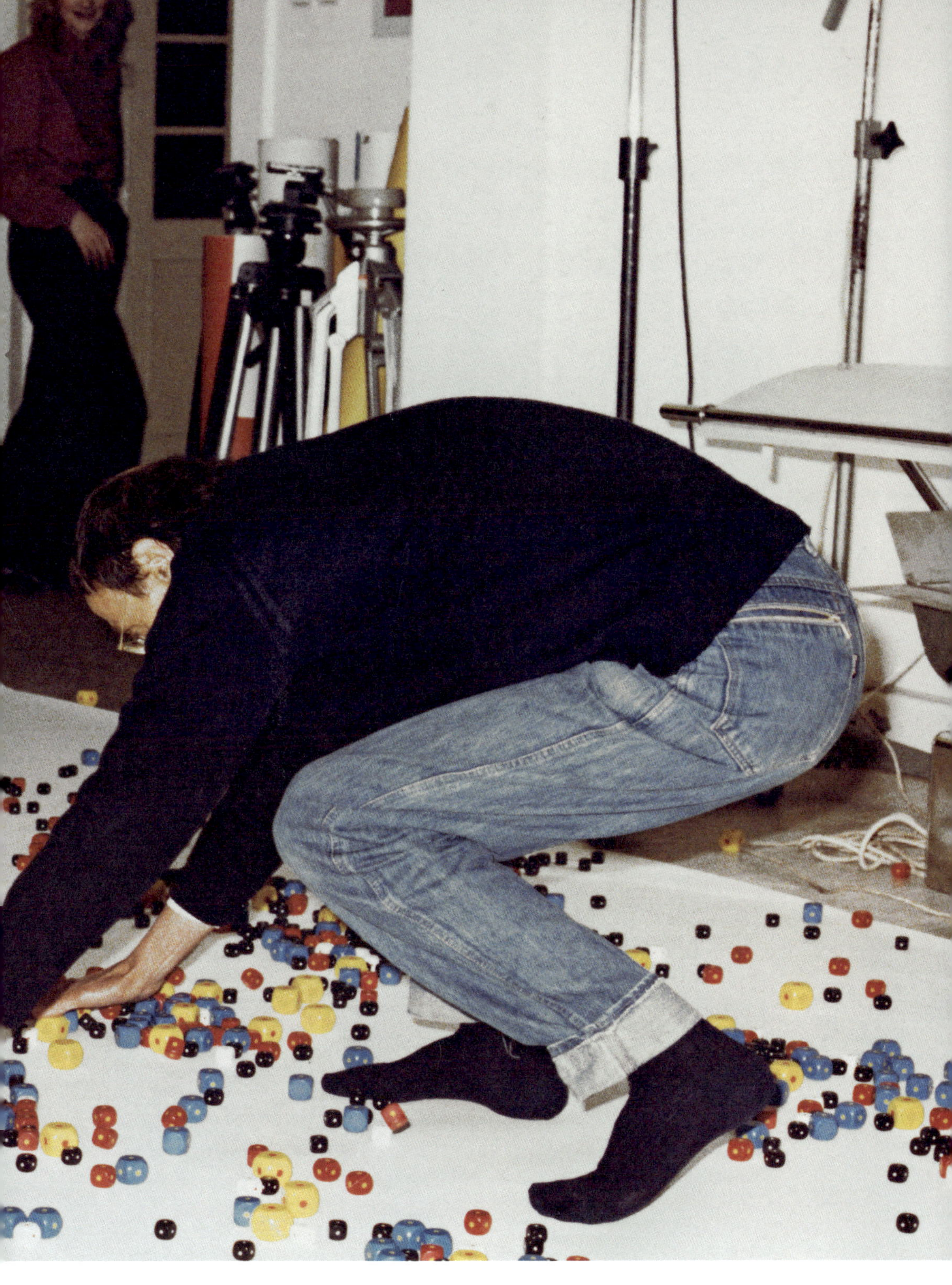

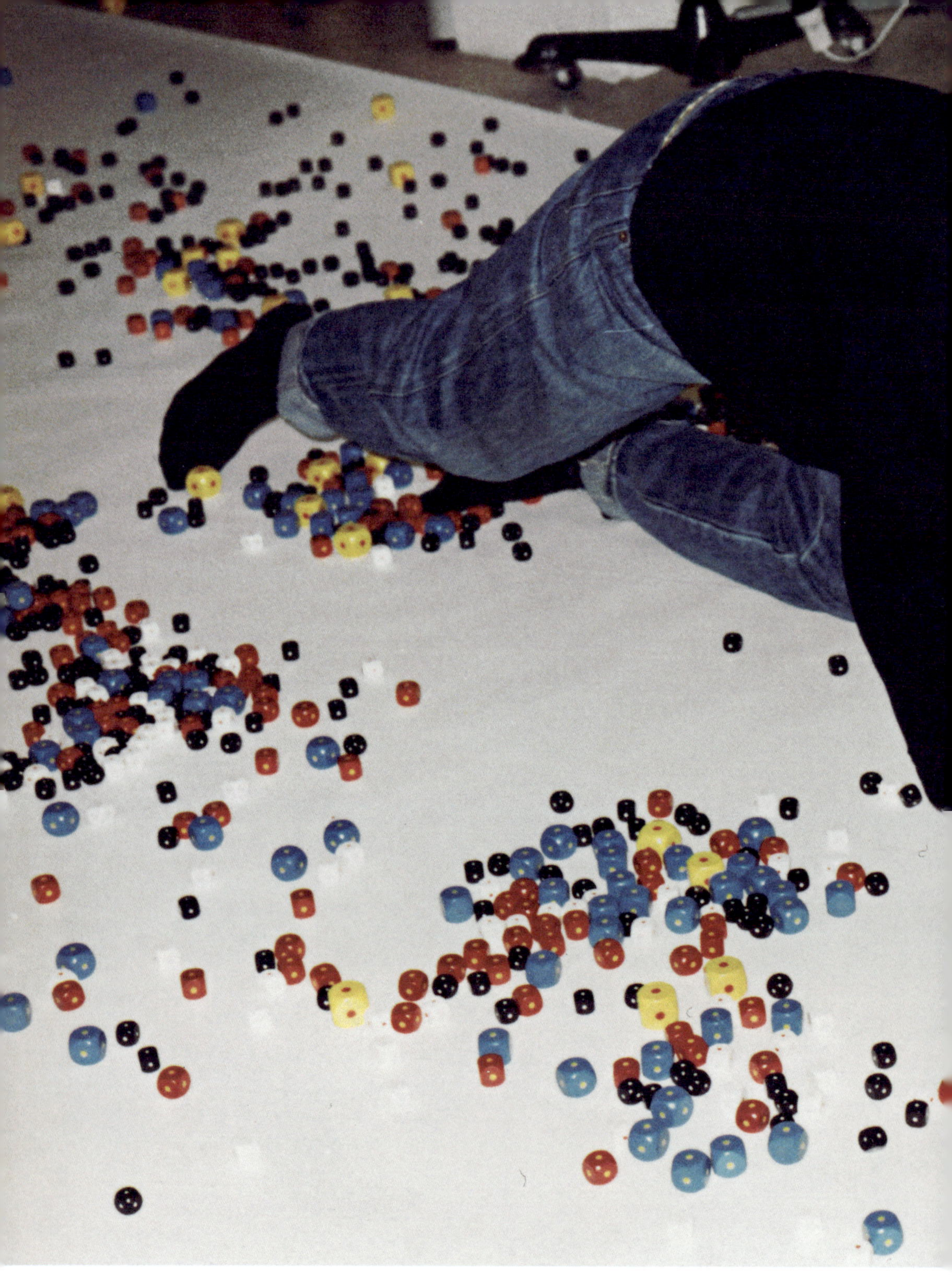

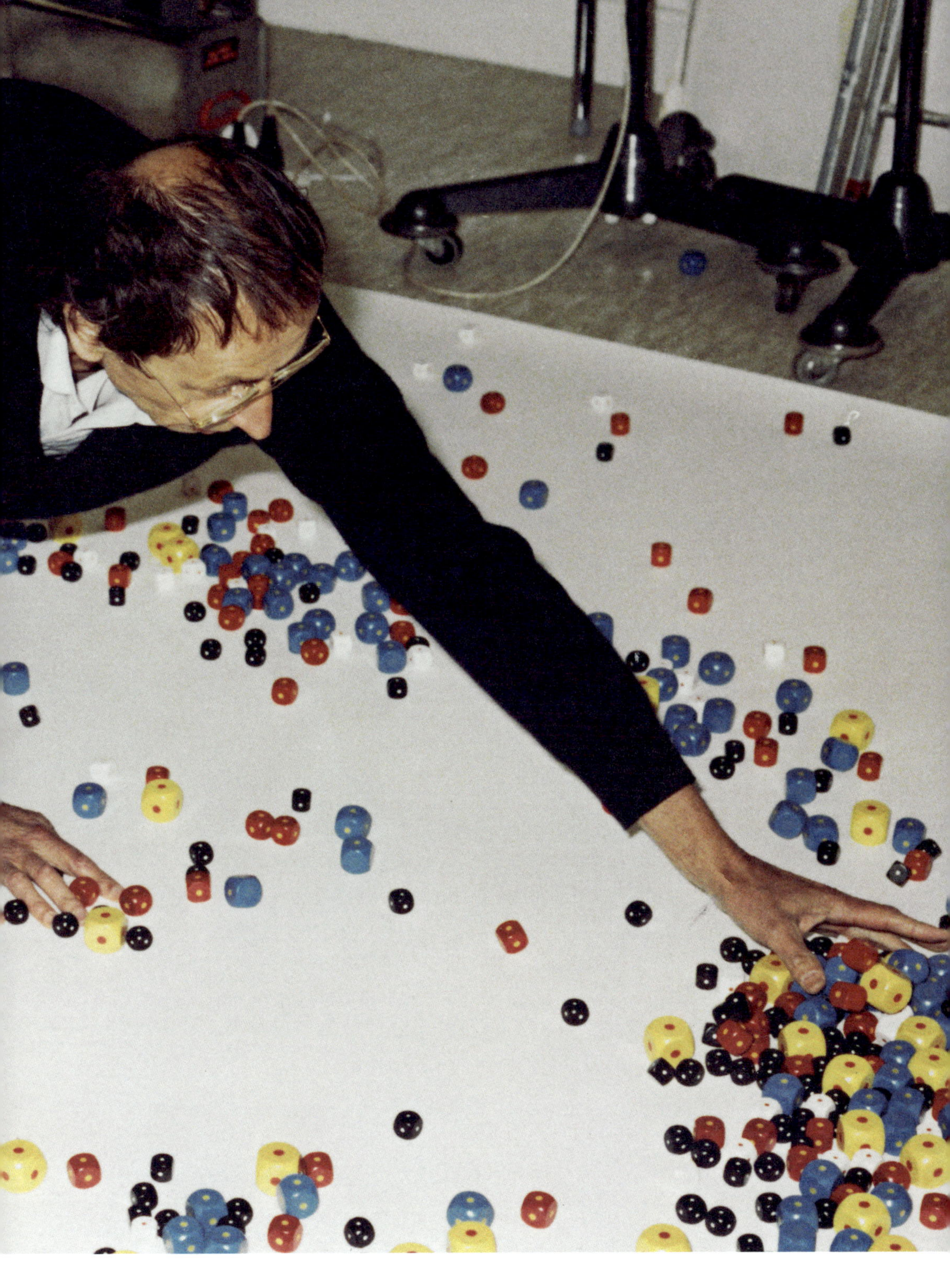

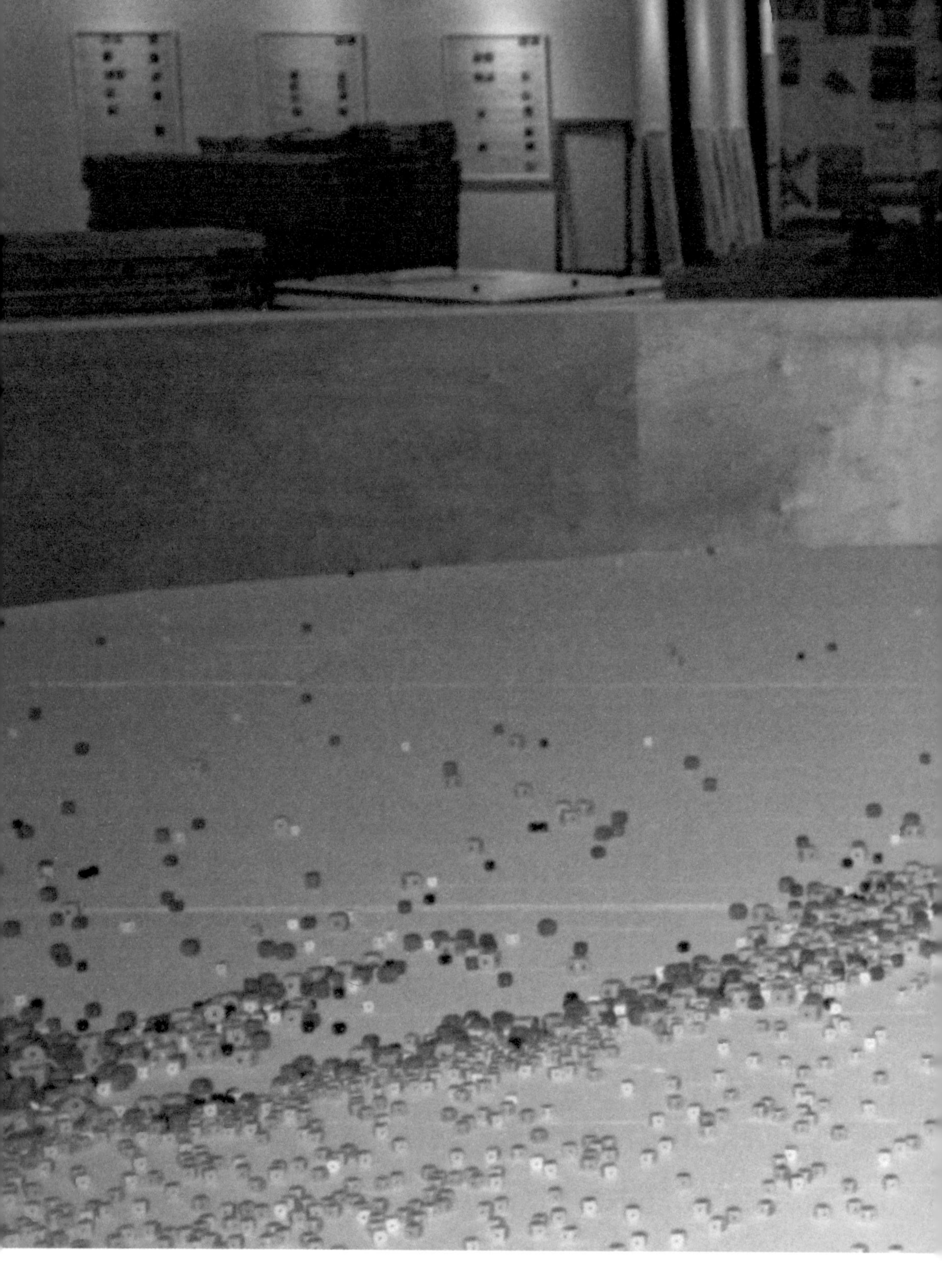

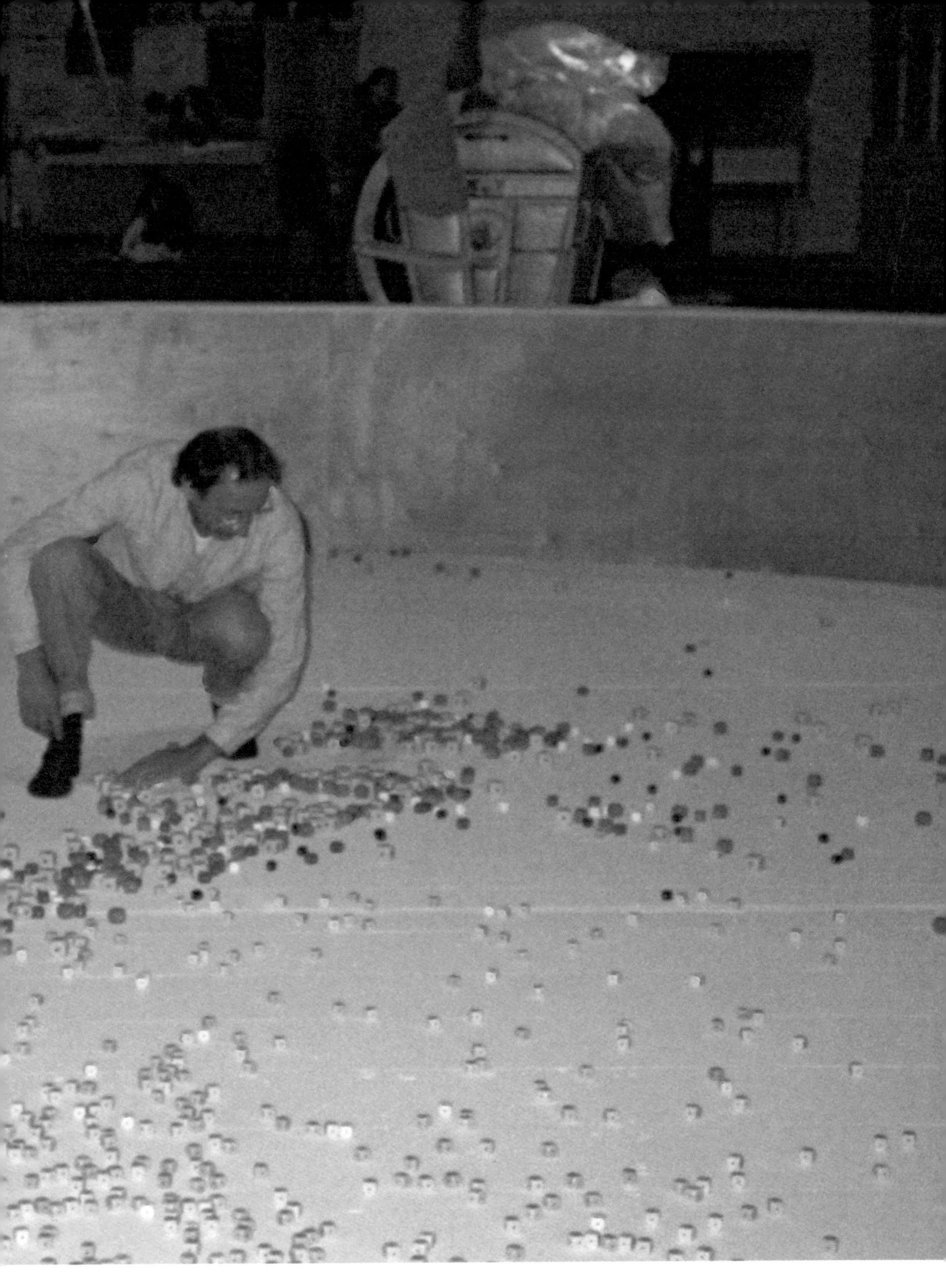

Robert Filliou placing the dices for *EINS. UN. ONE..* in the exhibition *Von hier aus*, Düsseldorf, 1984

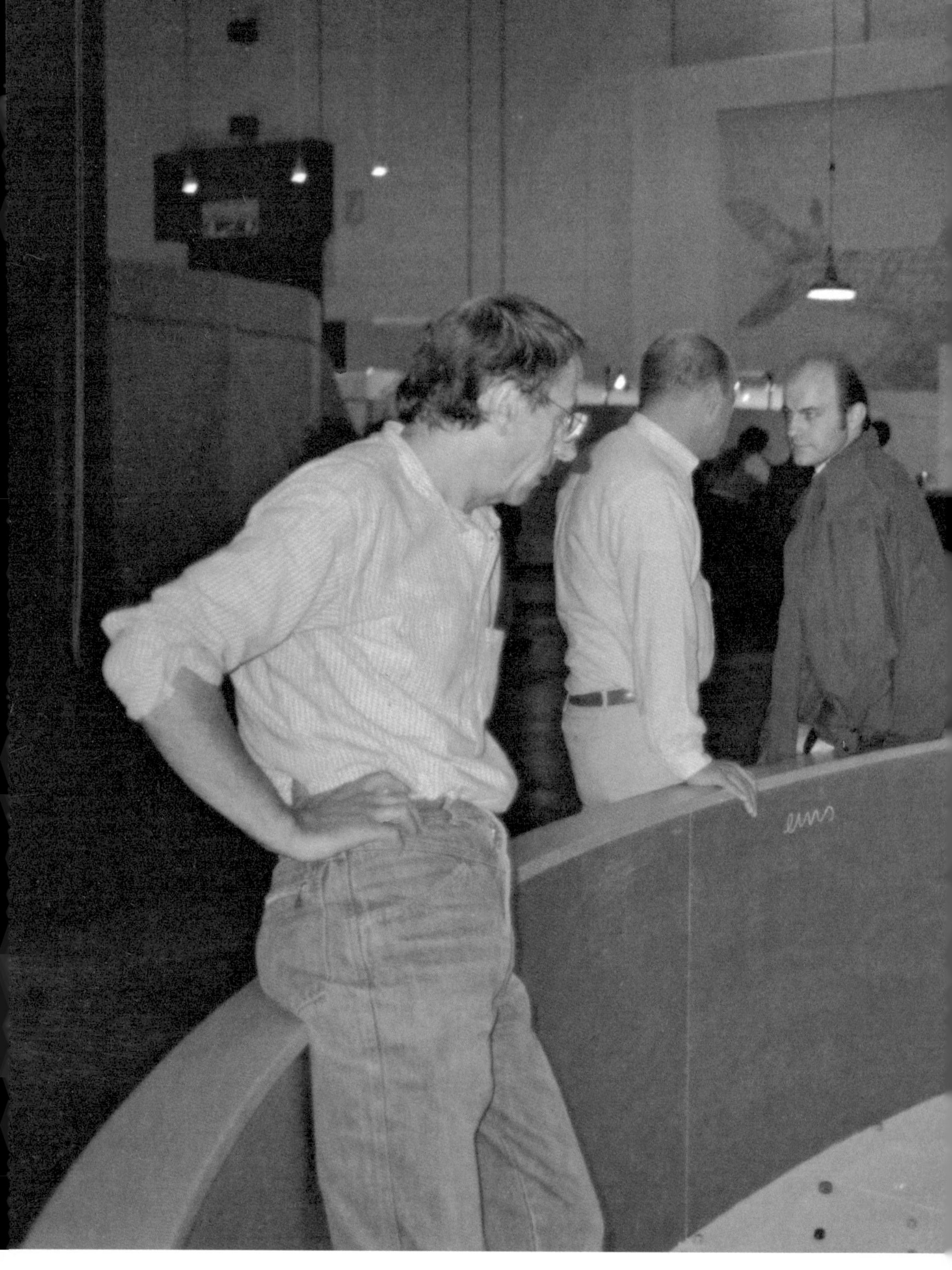

eins

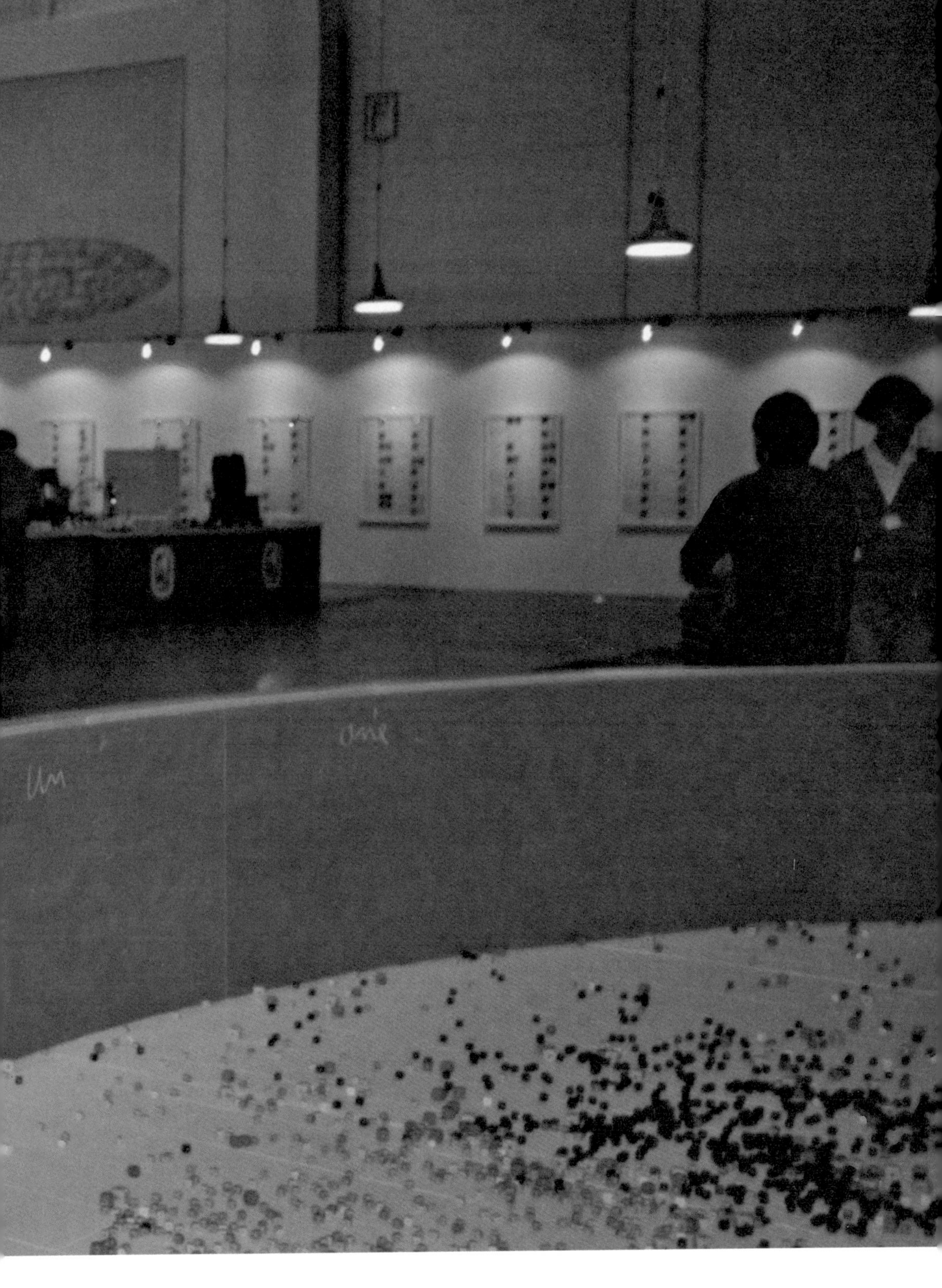

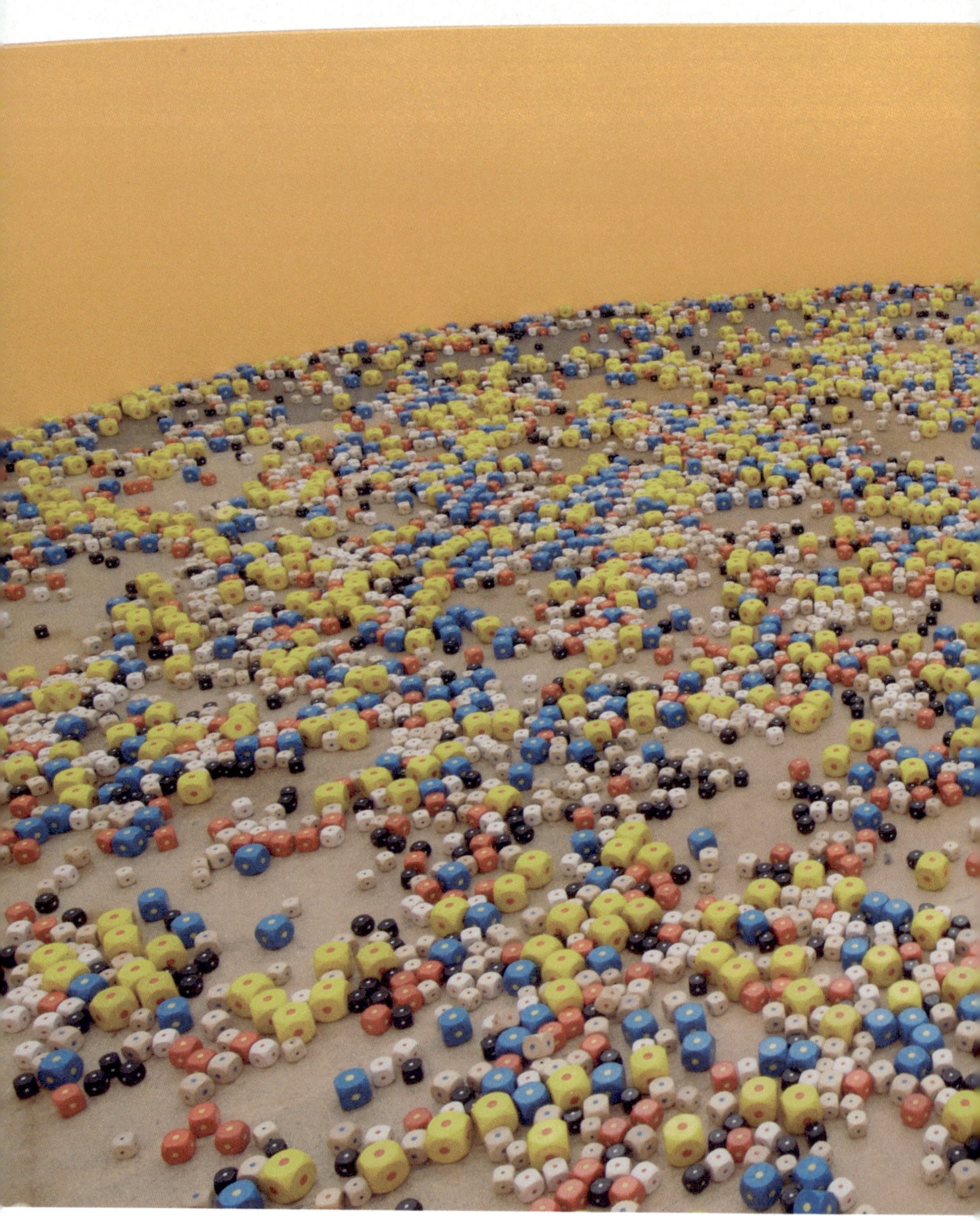

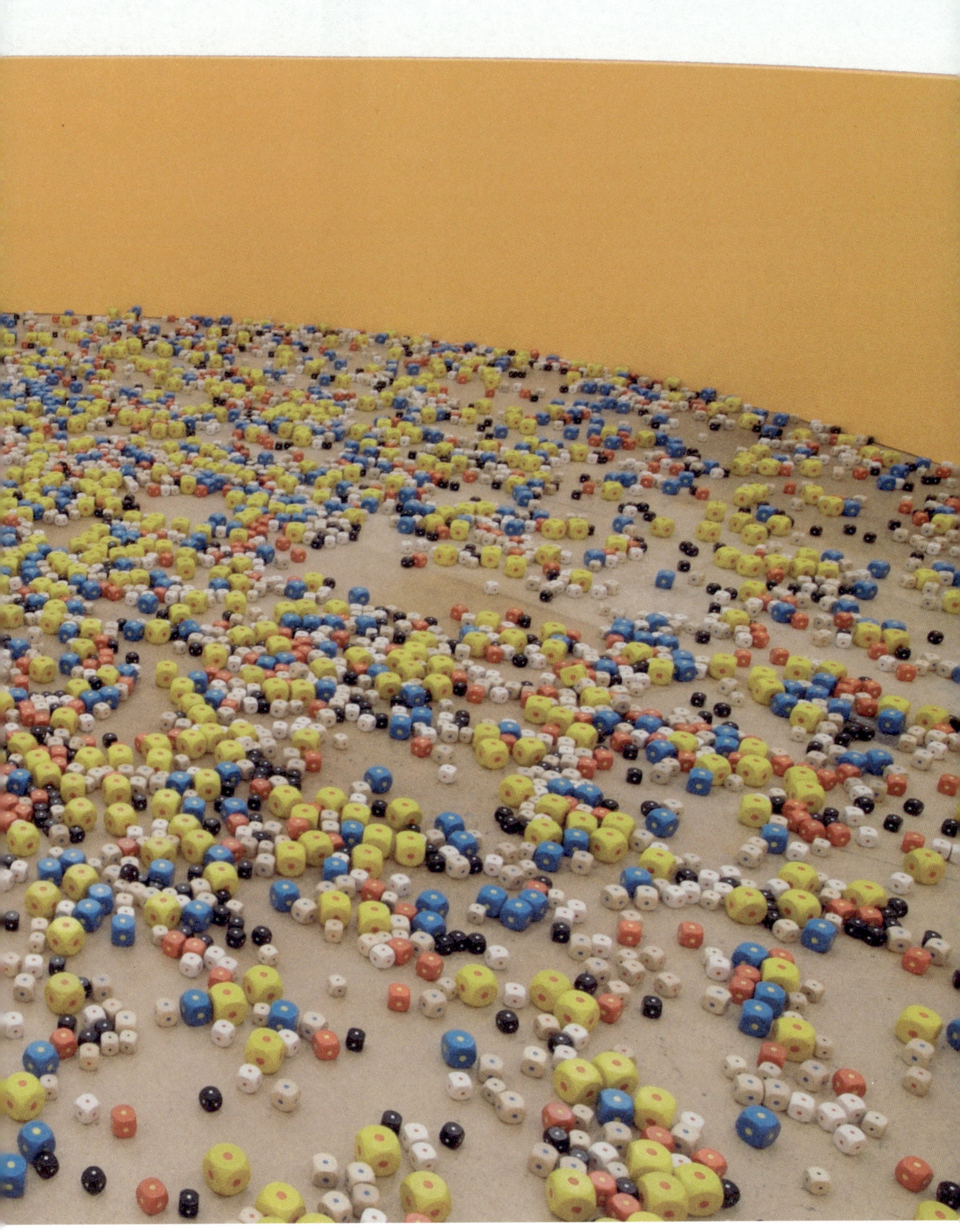

EINS. UN. ONE..., 1984, MAMCO Geneva

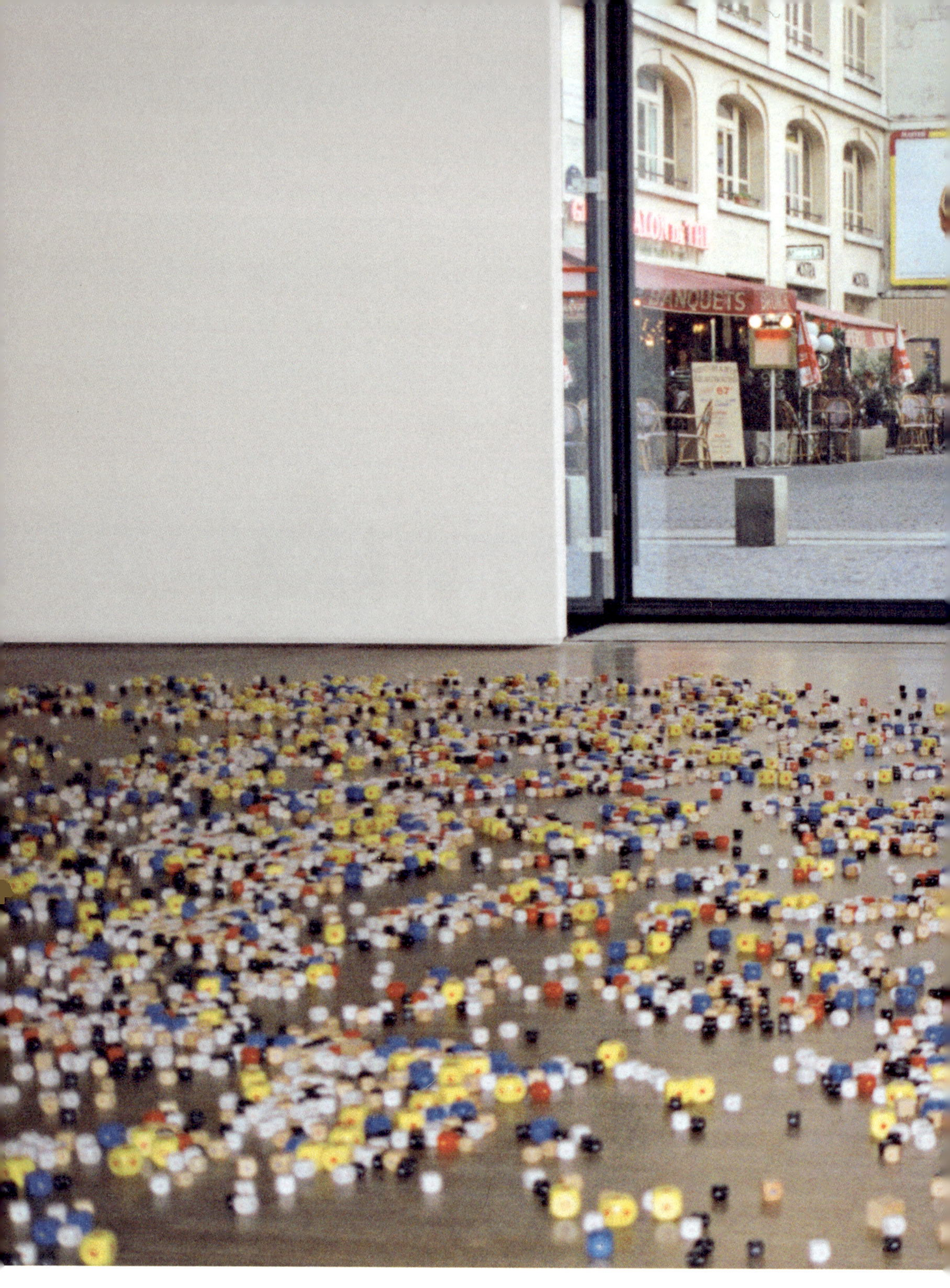

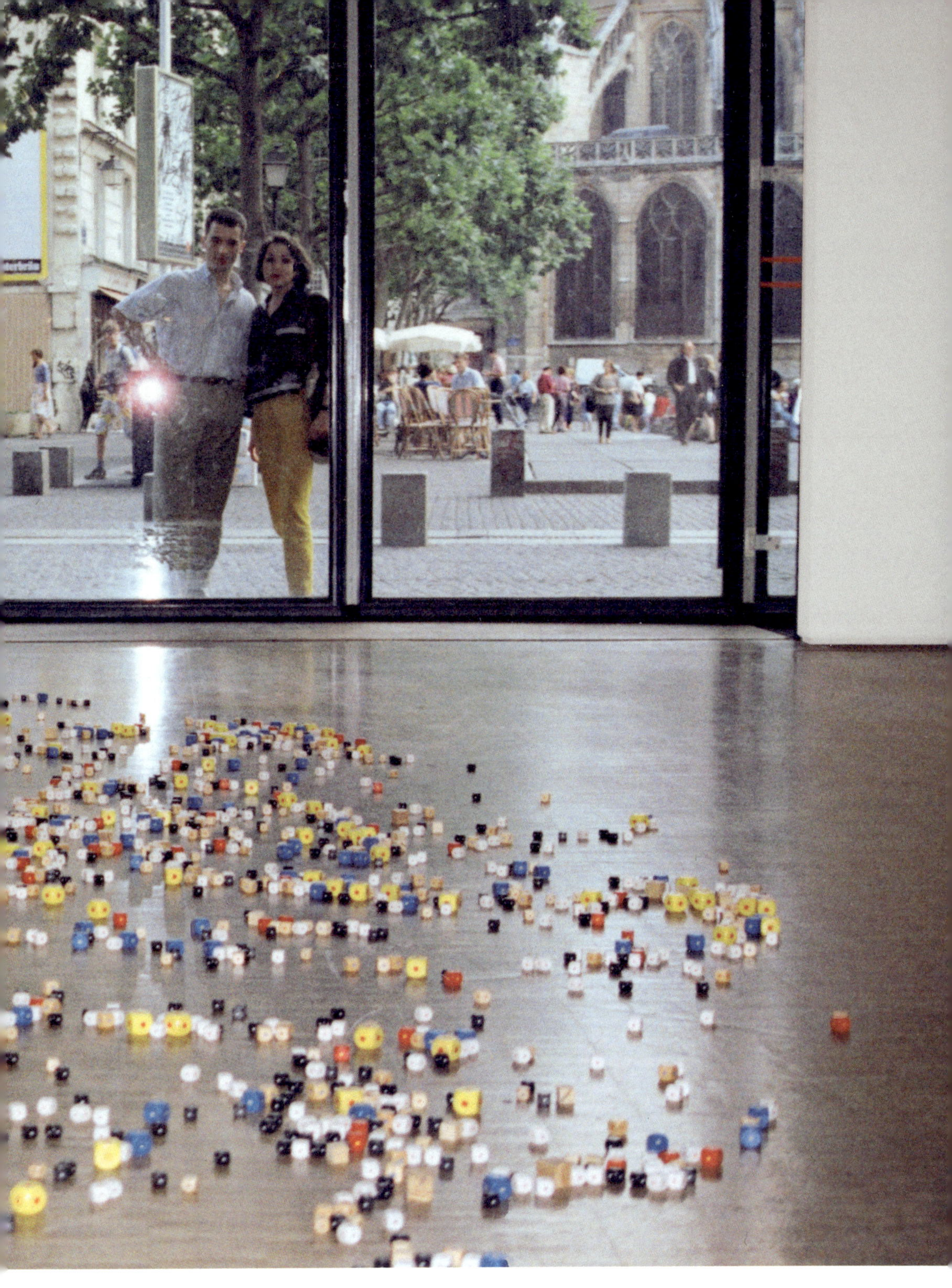

EINS. UN. ONE…, 1984, Centre Pompidou, Paris 1991

TABLE OF CONTENTS

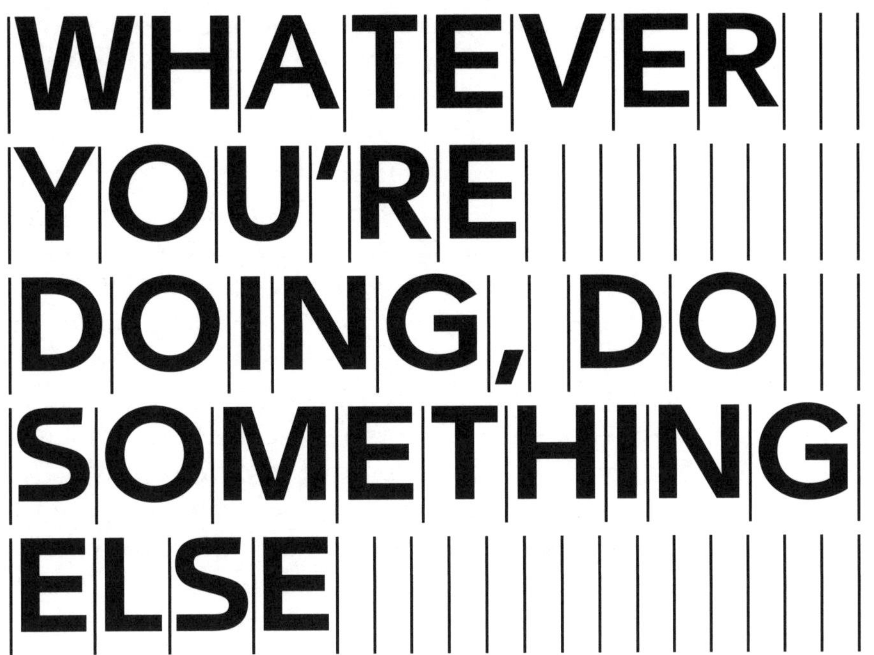

Michel Collet

Poet and playwright Robert Filliou held his first solo show, entitled *Poï-Poï*, at Galerie Köpcke in Copenhagen in 1961. For the occasion, he exhibited poems written on wrapping paper, and "poem-objects," experimenting with the endless potential offered by art as an alternative means of expression.[1] The show also included *L'Immortelle Mort du Monde/The Deathless Dying of the World*, a poster-format collage that, in a single work, blends three areas of Filliou's practice: poetry, stage writing, and the visual arts. "The poster contains the complete text of the play. The actors are represented by colors. For each actor, his text depends on the color of the actor immediately to his right… and this in turn on the fantasy of the ten actors as a whole. As well, sounds coming at random from offstage provide some directives. The play changes every night. Every time, besides, it could be made to run indefinitely… till the deathless dying of the world. It is an attempt to introduce on the stage the dynamic arbitrariness of our environment and our thoughts and emotions."[2]

A diagrammatic play, *L'Immortelle Mort du Monde/The Deathless Dying of the World* was published several years later in New York by Dick Higgins, the editor of *A Filliou Sampler*.[3] For all its playfulness, this work, a template for a dynamic theater piece, is a complex score that bears the hallmarks of the feedback and cybernetics theories developed in the 1950s. Filliou studied economics at the University of California following the end of the Second World War, the very time at which these new schools of scientific thought were emerging, and kept abreast of the latest theoretical developments as an avid reader of popular science writings.[4] Despite abandoning a fledgling career as an economist in 1954, he sustained a lifelong passion for logic and systems of thought. He was particularly fond of the works of Charles Fourier, the visionary French philosopher who argued that human desire and economic reality should not be mutually exclusive, describing him as "the nineteenth century thinker and Utopist who before Marx wrote and before Freud was born, succeeded in reconciling both."[5] An outspoken critic of the profit-driven market economy, Filliou developed the concept of "Poetic Economy,"[6] a model that would reconcile "the gnosis which is so happy, so light and economics which is so dismal"[7] and be in harmony with a world of creation and sensitive perception; a world, as Alexandre Koyré put it, "where we live, love, and die."[8]

Through his artistic practice, Filliou addressed concerns around the economy and social transformation, sometimes unexpectedly flipping established values on their head, such as when he celebrated the bankruptcy of *La Cédille qui Sourit*.[9] His work also reflected a primordial quest for spirituality, which led him to study Buddhist philosophy and practice meditation.[10] *L'Immortelle Mort du Monde/The Deathless Dying of the World* is a spiritual, spatialized, propositional adventure through which Filliou aimed to stimulate creativity among the performers. In fact, so firm was his belief in their individual creative capacities that he considered them to be co-authors.

With its conceptual power, Filliou's work has a distinctive quality. Tinged with laughter and a profound sense of humanity, it immediately situates the artist as a renegade who defies easy classification.[11] Was he a Conceptual artist? A member of the Fluxus movement? A non-artist? A poet? He preferred to talk in terms of philosophical art. Whether in Sauve (the village where he grew up in the Cévennes, southern France), Vancouver (when he worked at Western Front), Düsseldorf (where he and Daniel Spoerri lived with their friends), Flayosc, or Geneva, he embraced the banality of everyday life with it joys and occasional sorrows, challenged notions of art, and shunned pervasive materialism. He created fluid, lightweight objects with the meagerest of materials (bits of wood, dust, pieces of cardboard, nails, screws, or bricks), a method he flippantly called "*briquolage*."[12] He even asked himself the question "when is too much?"[13] It should be said that Filliou worked in precarious conditions, often in studios lent to him by friends, museums, or galleries. But none of this mattered to him. Because, as he said himself, "what matters most in the work of an artist is profound intuition."[14] Filliou's infectious sense of wonder allowed him to embrace the unpredictable with detachment because, at its core, "art is where you do your work, art is what we are doing."[15] Filliou and Marianne, his lifelong companion, lived through these years of destitution together.

The *Poï-Poï* exhibition held in the early 1960s was nevertheless a decisive turning point in Filliou's career, marking the start of a period of intense artistic output, as well as numerous publications and works of experimental poetry. Major pieces and several principles that would go on to shape his work came into being at this time, including the *Poïpoïdrome* (devised with Joachim Pfeufer, 1963), the notion of "Permanent Creation," *La Cédille qui Sourit* (founded with George Brecht, 1965–1968, the Eternal Network,[16] and the "Principle of Equivalence" ("Well made, badly made, not made: in terms of Permanent Creation, I suggest that these possibilities are equivalent.").[17]

Filliou readily expressed his admiration for "café-geniuses."[18] Like them, he saw himself as a genius without talent, working to create a constellation in constant flux, where concepts and works alike were born of intuition in a permanent movement akin to a game. Play was also central to his work on The Principles of Poetic Economy, according to which the aim was to move from "Work as Toil" to "Work as Play."[19] He also wrote: "I belong to this group of artists, or perhaps this generation of artists or this population of artists, since there have always been artists, who think they can change the world we live in, and I don't care if art doesn't exist as long as people are happy."[20]

Despite his prolific and diverse output, Filliou maintained that the visible part of his work was only a tiny fraction of a much bigger project: "99% of my work is unseen."[21] In fact, he preferred the more dynamic term "creativity" to the word "art," believing that it opened up a world beyond mere physical properties and suggested potential for emancipation. He was interested less in works of art themselves and more in the creative process and the associated receptive experience: "I do not believe that artistic activity involves the production of works of art as such. To create works of art is to engage in a process of exchange."[22]

The story of the self-taught artist Robert Filliou has often been told in writings and research on his creative process, so lacking in formal ostentatiousness is his output, a body of work that gently yet compellingly touches on questions of meaning, like a mind-opener[23] in the midst of the vastness of "the world as a whole."[24]

Notes

1   "Poets, even when they are published, have little or no public," in Robert Filliou, *Teaching and Learning as Performing Arts*, edited by Kasper König, Verlag Gebr. König, Cologne/ New York, 1970, p. 77.

2   Original text in English, from R. Filliou archives, not published.

3   Robert Filliou, *A Filliou Sampler*, Something Else Press, "A Great Bear Pamphlet" series New York, 1967.

4   Letter to Roger Tabanou, California, 1953, in *Robert Fillliou*, exhibition catalog, Centre Georges Pompidou, Paris, 1991, p. 25.

5   "The Principles of Poetic Economy is probably my longest research project—I have been working on it for some fifteen years. I dedicated The Principles of Poetic Economy to Fourier." In *Robert Filliou*, exhibition catalog, Sprengel-Museum, Hanover, Musée d'Art Moderne de la Ville de Paris, Kunsthalle Bern, Paris, 1984, p. 131.

6   Robert Filliou first considered writing a book on The Principles of Poetic Economy in 1966. He subsequently fleshed out his ideas in his 1970 book *Teaching and Learning as Performing Arts*.

7   *Robert Filliou*, Sprengel-Museum, Hanover, Musée d'Art Moderne de la Ville de Paris, Kunsthalle Bern, *op. cit.*, p. 132.

8   Alexandre Koyré, *Newtonian Studies*, Chapman & Hall, London, 1965.

9   "As you can see, we included the fact of our being bankrupt in La Fête Permanente. To us, this is an important element of the Eternal Network: including into it the harmful, painful or disagreeable things of life, as well as the pleasant, profitable ones." Robert Filliou, *Teaching and Learning as Performing Arts*, *op. cit.*, p. 203.

10   Robert Filliou contributed to the translation of *Le Chemin de la Grande Perfection* by Patrul Rinpoché, Padmakara, Saint-Léon-sur-Vézère, 1987.

11   "I have always refused to join a group," wrote Filliou in *Teaching and Learning as Performing Arts*, *op. cit.*, p. 52.

12   "*Briquolage* is in keeping with the ideal of 'Permanent Creation' that I have proposed to myself and to others, and which revolves around a secret relating to Permanent Creation: 'whatever you're doing (thinking), do (think) something else (…).'" In *Robert Fillliou*, Centre Georges Pompidou, *op. cit.*, p. 125. The term "*briquolage*" is a play on words combining "*bricolage*" (home improvement/makeshift work) and "*brique*" (brick).

13   Robert Filliou, cited by Alison Knowles, in *Assis tranquillement, ne faisant rien*, in *Robert Fillliou*, Centre Georges Pompidou *op. cit.*, p. 34.

14   Interview with Georg Jappe, 1984, cited in *Robert Filliou*, Brussels, Lebeer Hossmann, 1990, p. 72.

15   *Robert Fillliou*, Centre Georges Pompidou, *op. cit.*, p. 120.

16   "But also, over the month, we had developed the concept of the Fête Permanente, or Eternal Network," Robert Filliou, *Teaching and Learning as Performing Arts*, *op. cit.*, p. 203.

17   *Robert Filliou*, Sprengel-Museum, Hanover, Musée d'Art Moderne de la Ville de Paris, Kunsthalle Bern, *op. cit.*, p. 59.

18   "All of us are now sorts of café-geniuses. (…) [W]e have more ideas than possibilities of realizing them." Robert Filliou, *Teaching and Learning as Performing Arts*, *op. cit.*, p. 73.

19   *Robert Filliou*, Sprengel-Museum, Hanover, Musée d'Art Moderne de la Ville de Paris, Kunsthalle Bern, *op. cit.*, p. 131.

20   *Robert Filliou*, Brussels, Lebeer Hossmann, *op. cit.*, p 58.

21   Pierre Tilman, *Robert Filliou: Nationalité poète*, Les presses du réel, Dijon, 2007, p. 182.

22   Interview with Georg Jappe, 1984, cited in *Robert Filliou*, Brussels, Lebeer Hossmann, *op. cit.*, p. 72.

23   "A typical mind-opener to me would be, once I was with a Moroccan worker in France and he asked me for some samples of my work and I give him something of what we are doing and he said: 'Monsieur, vous êtes un zero'." *Robert Filliou*, Sprengel-Museum, Hanover, Musée d'Art Moderne de la Ville de Paris, Kunsthalle Bern, *op. cit.*, p. 110.

24   Robert Filliou in *Opus International*, Paris, No. 22, January 1971, p. 20.

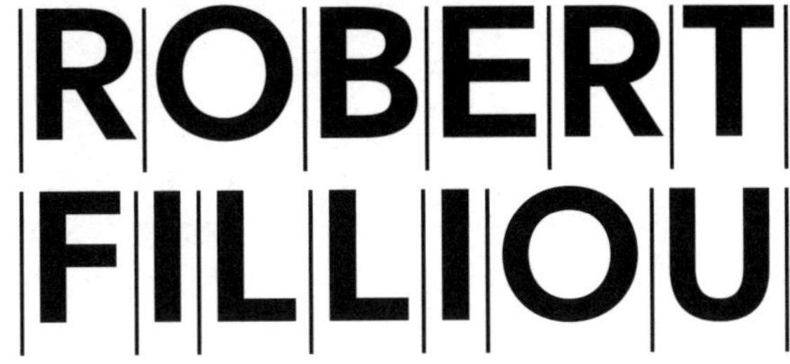

ROBERT FILLIOU

Sophie Costes

"EVEN THE TRAPEZE HAS A SHADOW"

Austrian writer Robert Musil died in exile in Geneva.[1] The city paid tribute to him with a bronze bust at the Plainpalais Cemetery, known as the "Cemetery of Kings,"[2] where he joined the writers Jorge Luis Borges, Alice Rivaz, and Rodolphe Toepffer. The inscription on this monument—"S'il y a un sens du réel, il doit y avoir aussi un sens du possible" ("If there is such a thing as a sense of reality, there must also be a sense of possibility")[3]—is the title of the fourth sub-chapter of *The Man Without Qualities*, an unfinished novel published between 1930 and 1943[4]. According to Marianne Filliou, it was Robert Filliou's favorite book, perhaps for this passage:

> But if there is such a thing as a sense of reality—and no one will doubt that it has its *raison d'être*—then there must also be something that one can call a sense of possibility. Anyone possessing it does not say, for instance: Here this or that has happened, will happen, must happen. He uses his imagination and says: Here such and such might, should or ought to happen. And if he is told that something is the way it is, then he thinks: Well, it could probably just as easily be some other way. So the sense of possibility might be defined outright as the capacity to think how everything could 'just as easily' be, and to attach no more importance to what is than to what is not. It will be seen that the consequences of such a creative disposition may be remarkable, and unfortunately they not infrequently make the things that other people admire appear wrong and the things that other people prohibit permissible, or even make both appear a matter of indifference. Such possibilitarians live, it is said, within a finer web, a web of hazy imaginings, fantasy and the subjunctive mood.[5]

For Musil, the space between reality and possibility was occupied by imagination and dreams—and we know that Filliou considered imagination and innocence to be among the driving forces behind art. The idea that things could be some "other" way is a key theme in *L'Autrisme*, the 1962 action poem in which he conceptualized his concept of "Permanent Creation"—the notion according to which everything is in constant motion and open to challenge. Indeed, Filliou's mantra—"Whatever you're thinking, think something else/Whatever you're doing, do something else"—is an "ode to creativity and action."[6]

Musil's proposition to "attach no more importance to what is than to what is not" (and its corollary, "something real means no more than something imagined") could conceivably be considered a "principle of equivalence"—something that would become a key theme in Filliou's work. After all, was not Filliou, like Musil's Ulrich, a "possibilitarian": a man who sided with the dreamers, the losers, the Dharma Bums, relying on the power of poetry and dreams to try to change the world? And when, during a 1965 performance at New York's Café Go-Go, Filliou revealed the Absolute Secret of Permanent Creation—"Desire nothing, decide nothing, choose nothing, be aware of yourself, stay awake, CALMLY SEATED, DO NOTHING"—was he not channeling the spirit of the "man without qualities"?

Like Musil, Filliou devoted part of his time to writing for the stage. The former's sense of irony and "amused idleness"[7] were matched by the latter's irreverence and systematic rejection of conventional wisdom. But while Ulrich decided to "take a year's leave from his life" in a disenchanted world, Filliou sought to re-enchant the world.

ROBERT FILLIOU AND SWITZERLAND

During his lifetime, Filliou's work was shown in several solo exhibitions in Switzerland, including at Galerie Handschin (Basel, 1969), Kunstraum Medici (Solothurn, 1973), and Galerie Marika Malacorda (Geneva, 1978 and 1982). He also took part in a number of group shows, including *Pantogrammes* at Galerie Handschin (1976, with André Thomkins, FIG. 1) and *Spiralen & Progressionen* at the Kunstmuseum Luzern (1978, with Paul Klee, Richard Long, Mario Merz, Bruce Naumann, and Robert Smithson, among others).

The retrospective exhibition *The Eternal Network* opened at the Sprengel Museum, Hanover, in 1984. After a period at the Musée d'Art Moderne de Paris,[8] it moved to its final destination, the Kunsthalle Bern, where it closed in 1985. The exhibition poster

[FIG. 2] showed Filliou in high spirits alongside Marianne and their daughter Marceline, the trio playing perfect tourists on a boat gliding across an underground lake (perhaps the lake in the Saint-Léonard Cavern).

Filliou was a regular exhibitor at Galerie Marika Malacorda in Geneva.[9] He took part in the gallery's inaugural show, *What's the Time?*, which opened on November 19, 1976 [FIG. 3]. Curated by John M Armleder, it included works by Ben, Joseph Beuys, George Brecht, Giuseppe Chiari, Ludwig Gosewitz, Hal Hansen, Allan Kaprow, Alison Knowles, Arthur Köpcke, Nam June Paik, Dieter Roth, Daniel Spoerri, André Thomkins, Wolf Vostell, and Robert Watts. It was accompanied by a 1964 text in which Brecht sought to define what Fluxus was or was not.

Filliou's first solo show at Galerie Marika Malacorda opened on January 28, 1978. It featured 12 visual palindromes. The drawings, entitled *Mensonges de Lapalisse (Palindromes visuels n° I à XII)*, were executed in ink pad, chalk, and black pencil on paper from a spiral-bound notebook. These works were acquired by Geneva-based collector and MAMCO founder André L'Huillier. They went on display at the museum when it opened, remaining there until 2013.

A "lapalissade" is an obvious truth. Here, Filliou drew a parallel between lapalissades and visual palindromes,[10] except that, in this case, the "truths" were lies: his palindromes were not perfect and the visuals they contained were not equivalent. The drawings he reproduced were, ostensibly, visual signatures of artists such as Paul Klee, Kazimir Malevich, Marcel Duchamp, Pablo Picasso, and Jackson Pollock. But, taken as a whole, they were very much an approximation—according to the Principle of Equivalence, they were "badly made." Filliou, presenting himself as an expert, gave three possible definitions of the term "*Mensonge de La Palisse*" ("Lapalissian Lie"), supposedly taken from the French dictionary *Micro Robert: Dictionnaire du Français Primordial*.

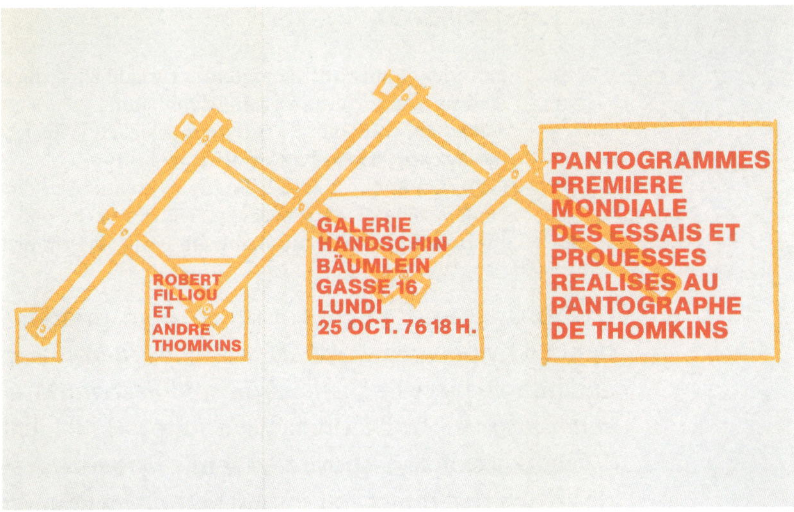

[FIG.1]   *Pantogrammes*, 1976
Coll. MAMCO, legs Gérald et Muriel Minkoff-Olesen

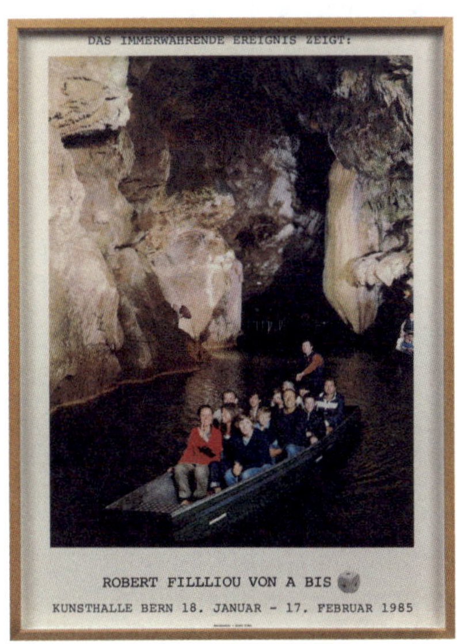

[FIG.2]   *Das Immerwährende Ereignis zeigt: Robert Filliou von a bis d*, 1984
Coll. MAMCO, legs Gérald et Muriel Minkoff-Olesen

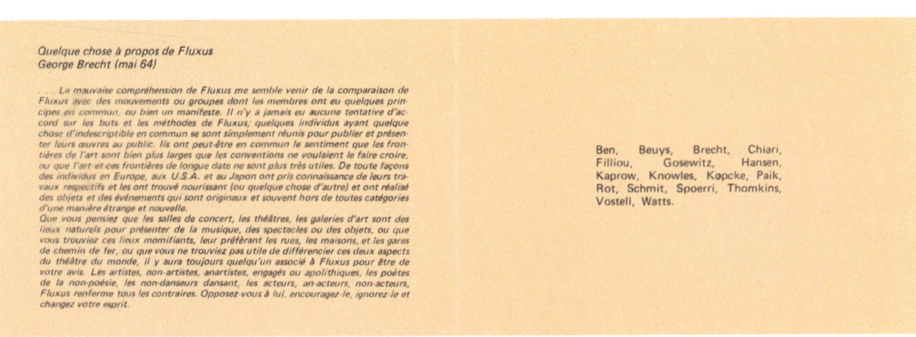

[FIG.3]   *What's the Time?*, 1976
Coll. MAMCO, legs Gérald et Muriel Minkoff-Olesen

1   an indisputably untrue statement made with the intention of not mis-
     leading (e.g. the origin of this definition)
2   a laughably obvious untruth (if it is sick, it is healthy), which may simply
     be the expression of a paradoxical reality
3   (slang) an unquestionably bogus assertion by a state body summoned to
     explain an abuse of power (e.g. "the lies of the police," François Dufrêne)
     —Micro Robert: Dictionnaire Du Français Primordial, P. 660[11]

Dictionaries were a frequent source of inspiration for Filliou, as evidenced by his 1962 work *Sémantique générale* (General Semantics) and his 1981 piece *Le Dictionnaire comme scénario – version lilllllliputienne intégrale* (The Dictionary as a Script – Full Lilllllliputian Version). "Why a dictionary? Above all, I think, Robert was seduced by the little arrows that direct you somewhere else whenever you think you've already arrived (that's the relative secret of Permanent Creation): sometimes in the opposite direction, sometimes to a dead end. Robert is a man of arrows and cedillas, of little arrows and cedillas and circles."[12]

Between September 13 and October 17, 1982, Galerie Marika Malacorda played host to Filliou's *Briquolages*.[13] This series, which he began creating in the early 1980s, featured the "brick" as a key component:

> Materials give me my ideas, not the other way around. More often than not, I start with whatever I have at hand and then, as I use that thing, an idea might come to me (…) I love bricks, and the contrast between the weight of a brick and the lightness of the spirit is something that interests me. So that's where it all began. It was only afterwards that I called it *Briquolage*…[14]

The invitation card [FIG. 4] features the two faces of Janus bordered by two bricks: one with holes (*should holes be plugged?*) and one without holes (*should holes be dug?*). This composition, which Filliou ironically named *Full-Employment Sculpture*, was accompanied by a comment: "in every village, every neighborhood, some dig, some plug." The text circles back to one of the *One-Minute Scenarios* (1965) devised by Brecht and Filliou during their time at *La Cédille qui sourit*, some of which were captured on 16 mm film by Bob Guiny.[15]

Briquolage 1 is a matrix that has already given birth to *Brickings and Kueens No. 1* and *Brickings and Kueens No. 2* (1983), as well as to numerous other characters. All endeavor, all discourse is *bricolage*. Taking the expression literally, I gained immense pleasure from (trying to) give wings to a material as majestically down-to-earth as brick.[16]

To give this material a lighter touch, Filliou added an extra "l" to his name—so that it would have three "l's" (the letter "l" sounds like "aile" in French, which means "wing")—when signing some of his *Briquolages*.[17] The magnificent sculpture *5 brickKINGS & KUEENS* [FIG. 5] was included in the exhibition at Galerie Marika Malacorda, where it was acquired by André L'Huillier and subsequently held at MAMCO until 2013.

It was John M Armleder who introduced Filliou to Malacorda:

Filliou was incredibly funny. You never really knew what he was doing: he was part-poet, he liked to drink, he had this desire to avoid being categorized in any way. He had no yearning for success—indeed, success was of no concern to an artist of his kind. For Beuys, success was a matter of chance. Maciunas thought along similar lines, according no importance to the artist's worth... Filliou made this envelope, which in fact was a postcard: *Envelope – A Postcard by Robert Filliou* (1976, Figs 6, 7). He took the idea of a postcard and flipped it on its head. I think there were other projects that never saw the light of day. He came to Ecart but exhibited at Marika's gallery soon after. Robert hardly ever came to Geneva. He didn't go anywhere by choice unless someone took him...[18]

In Geneva, Filliou also met Tony Morgan, a performer and photographer who at the time was making 16 mm films. *Double Happening* (1970) depicts Filliou and Emmet Williams performing in a toilet, while in *Düsseldorf ist ein guter Platz zu schlafen*, filmed in 1972, the artist is shown lying on the cobblestones of the German city.

In 1971, Filliou met the Geneva-based artist couple Gérald Minkoff and Muriel Olesen at the home of the artist Armand Schulthess.

Filliou was there without Marianne. He was staying with Spoerri, who at the time was living with Ingeborg Lüscher, whom Schulthess was in love with. Schulthess was an ageless figure (although he was getting on in years) who wore a turban around his head and hung scraps of tin cans inscribed with hieroglyphic

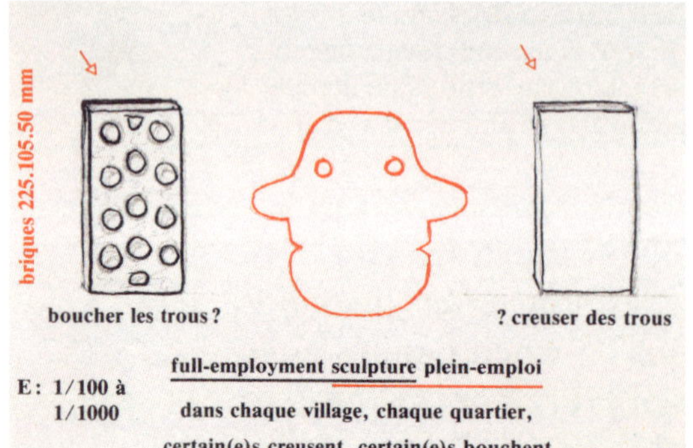

[FIG. 4]   *Full-employment Sculpture*, 1982
Coll. MAMCO, Ecart Archives

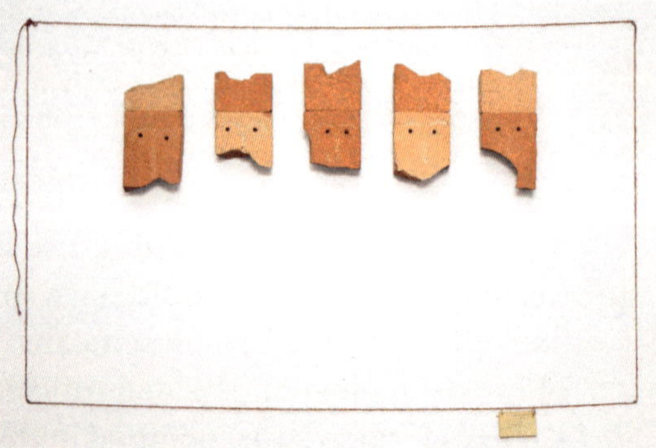

[FIG. 5]   *5 brickKINGS & KUEENS,* 1982
Carved bricks, string, paper; 84 × 131.5 cm
Coll. Renée L'Huillier

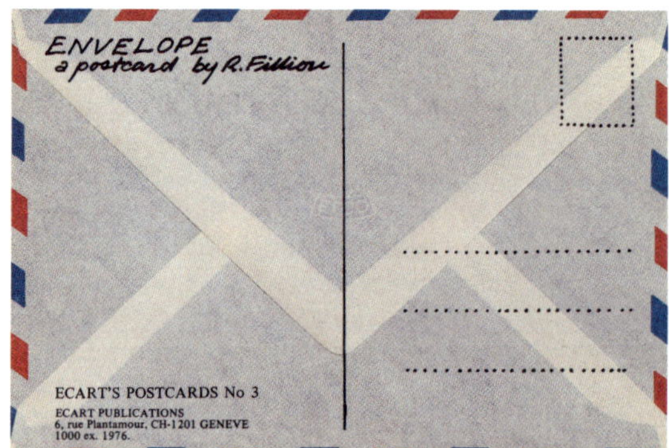

[FIG. 6]   *Envelope – A Postcard by Robert Filliou,* 1976
Printed envelope, 11.5 × 16 cm, 1'000 ex., ed. Ecart
Coll. MAMCO Collection, don Christian Bernard

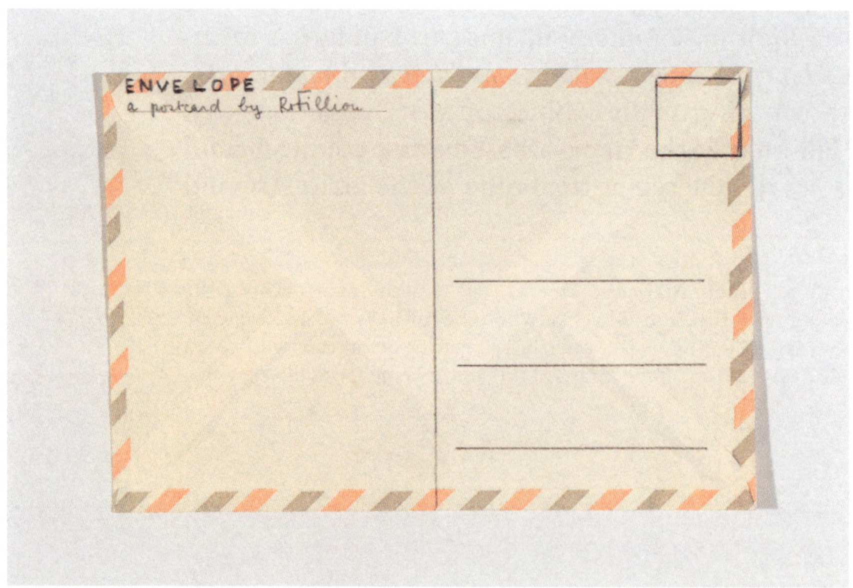

[FIG. 7]   *Envelope – A Postcard by Robert Filliou,* 1976
Pencil on envelope, 11.4 × 16.3 cm
Coll. MAMCO, legs Gérald et Muriel Minkoff-Olesen

writing from trees. Ingeborg "discovered" him when she drove past his property and saw all the things he'd hung from the tree branches…That day, Gérald had come to see Spoerri because he wanted to hold an exhibition at Galerie Bonnier. That's where we met Filliou. I remember Spoerri lifting me through a window frame to get inside the house. So I was "off my feet," so to speak, when I saw Filliou for the first time…[19]

A number of pieces by Minkoff and Olesen, as well as works by Filliou, were bequeathed to the MAMCO collection in 2021. These items include a black-and-white photograph of Minkoff and Filliou in a store, taken by Olesen in 1974 [FIG. 8]. The collection also includes articles documenting a collective work entitled *Parlez ! le concombre vous écoute*. This set—two drawings and a photograph of Thomkins working on the piece—also dates from 1974 and was shown at the Ecart retrospective held at MAMCO in 1997 (Figs 9, 10, 11). The catalog features a description of the project:

> Minkoff [with input from Filliou] set about building an object with a motor powered by the vinegar from a pickle. This object was then combined with a cutout paper ear and a magnetic-card audio recorder (which could record a few seconds of audio on each length of tape) that had been picked up during a trip to London. This work by Minkoff, produced following a conversation with Filliou, is entitled *Parlez ! le concombre vous écoute*. It was used to record the words of willing participants, which the artist then played back, in random order, during his performances [FIG. 12].[20]

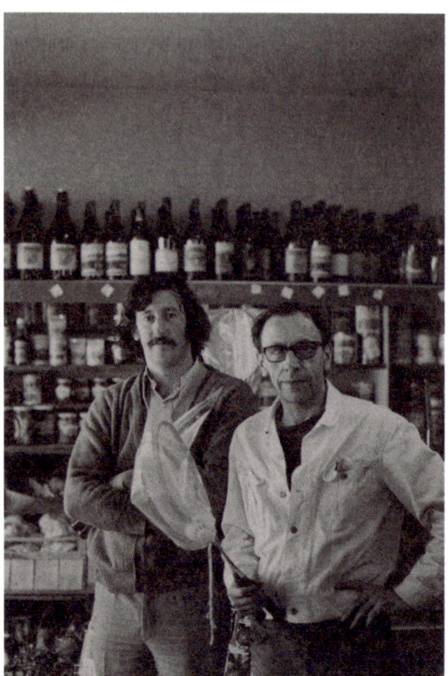

[FIG. 8] Muriel Olesen, *Robert Filliou and Gérald Minkoff*, 1974
Coll. MAMCO, legs Gérald et Muriel Minkoff-Olesen

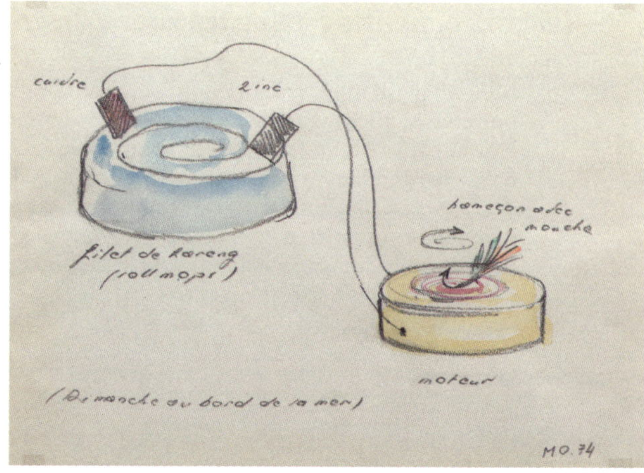

[FIG. 9] Muriel Olesen, *Dimanche au bord de la mer*, 1974
Pencil and watercolor on paper, 24 × 32 cm (unframed)
Coll. MAMCO, legs Gérald et Muriel Minkoff-Olesen

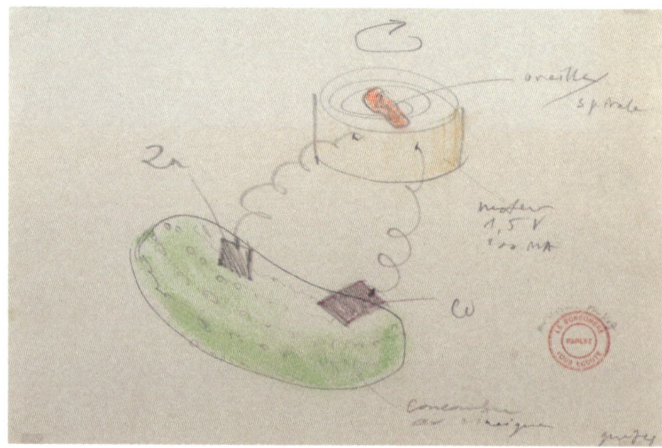

[FIG. 10] Robert Filliou et Gérald Minkoff, *Parlez!*
Le concombre vous écoute, 1974
Colored pencil, graphite, rubber stamp on paper;
26 × 38 cm
Coll. MAMCO, legs Gérald et Muriel Minkoff-Olesen

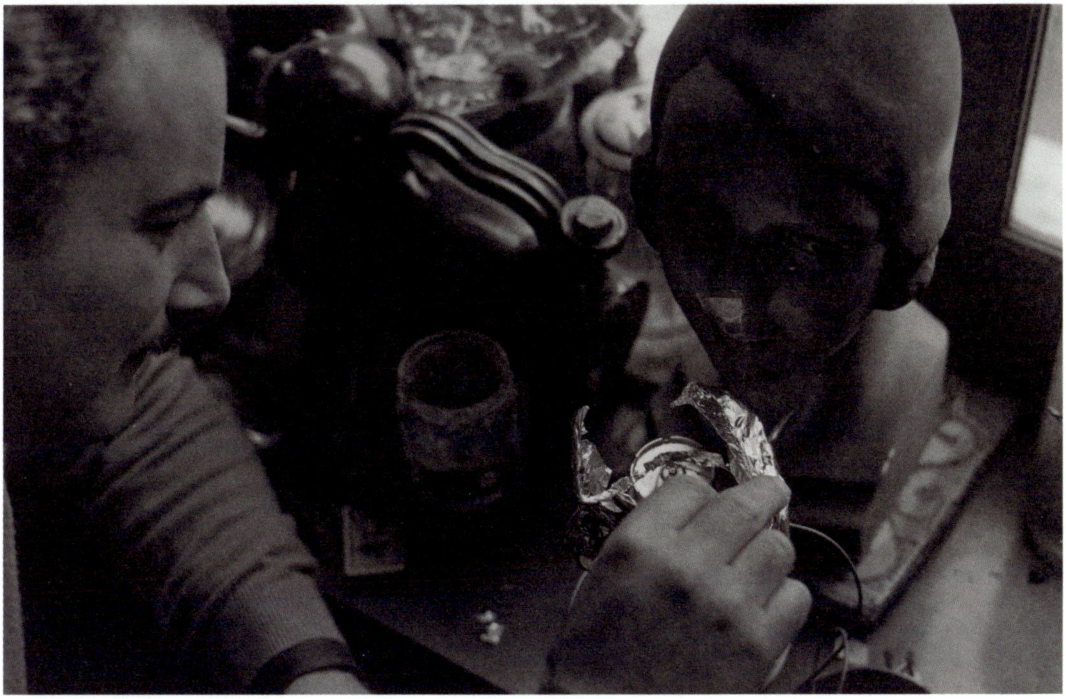

[FIG. 11] Muriel Olesen, *André Thompkins working on the motor of Parlez!*
Le concombre vous écoute
Coll. MAMCO, legs Gérald et Muriel Minkoff-Olesen

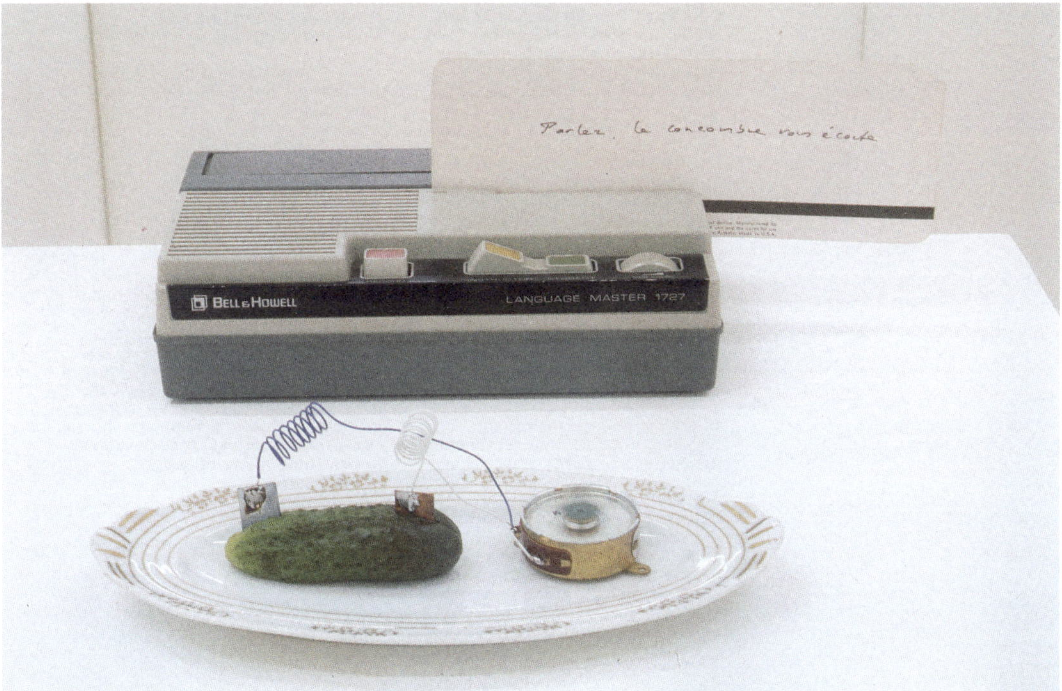

[FIG. 12] Marianne Filliou, Robert Filliou, Muriel Olesen, Gérald Minkoff, *Parlez! le concombre vous écoute*, 1974
Bell & Howell machine, punched cards, cucumber, electrodes
Coll. MAMCO, legs Gérald et Muriel Minkoff-Olesen

Notes

1   Musil died in 1942 in Geneva, where he had been living in hardship since 1938. His ashes were scattered in the Arve River, near Mont Salève, by his wife.

2   This cemetery is where famous Genevans, as well as notable outsiders who died in the city, are buried.

3   Robert Musil, *The Man Without Qualities*, Vol. 1, Secker & Warburg, London, 1953, p. 20.

4   The English translation was published between 1953 and 1961.

5   *Ibid.*, p. 20.

6   Robert Filliou, *Théâtre incomplet, AAREVUE 1969–1987*, reproduced in *Small Noise* No. 1, 1999, Issue No. 169–70.

7   This phrase was originally coined by Michel Collet.

8   Pierre Cabannes was enthusiastic about the exhibition: "The whole is so rich, so varied, that the effect is nothing short of staggering; yet everything Filliou invents remains casual, light, perishable, and utterly foreign to the craft, to learned art. His is a poetic, playful world crafted by a do-it-yourselfer—a world designed to move, to travel, to be transformed. 'Whatever you're doing, do something else,' says Filliou. And that is precisely what he keeps doing: making things that are well made, badly made, or not made at all." Pierre Cabannes, "Les 'choses' de Robert Filliou," in *Le Matin*, November 17–18, 1984, reproduced in *Robert Fillliou* [sic], exhibition catalog, Centre Pompidou, Paris, 1991, p. 130. Our translation.

9   An anthology of the gallery's first 10 exhibitions, entitled *Marika Malacorda Genève – 10 expositions 1976–1978*, was published in 1978 (Ecart, Geneva). In the foreword, Malacorda described her vision of a "gallery that was creative and informative in its identity and practice. So, wherever possible, I invited artists to be physically present and to create new works, installations or performances on site, so that visitors could interact directly with them." Our translation.

10   The palindrome arguably became an established feature of the Geneva art scene in 1969, when John M Armleder, Claude Rychner, and Patrick Lucchini chose "Ecart" ("Trace" backward) as the name for their collective. The artist Gérald Minkoff, a friend of Filliou, was a master "palindromographer": he created 350 palindromes between 1970 and 1997, the year in which *Tir, cet écrit* was published by MAMCO.

11   Here, Filliou took his "definitions" from the concise version of this dictionary for French learners.

12   Robert Filliou, *The Secret of Permanent Creation*, exhibition catalog, Museum of Contemporary Art Antwerp (M HKA), 2016, p. 9.

13   The term *"briquolage"* is a play on words combining *"bricolage"* (home improvement/makeshift work) and *"brique"* (brick).

14   "Extrait d'une interview de Robert Filliou par Georg Jappe" in *Robert Fillliou* [sic], Centre Pompidou, *op. cit*, p. 125. Our translation.

15   The *One-Minute Scenarios* were published in: George Brecht and Robert Filliou, *Games at the Cedilla, or the Cedilla Takes Off*, Something Else Press, New York, 1967. The idea was to film them as sketches for broadcast on television. They were translated into French, somewhat crudely, by Richard Tialans and published in *AAREVUE* in September 1972.

16   Marianne Filliou Archives, quoted in *Robert Fillliou* [sic], Centre Pompidou, *op. cit*. Our translation.

17   "Here is my proposed invitation card; the idea is to make a postcard that can be used later (years later) for correspondence. Please note that I now spell my name 'Fillliou,' with three 'l's.' Handwritten letter from Robert Filliou to Marika Malacorda, August 30, 1982, Malacorda Archives. Our translation.

18   Conversation with John M. Armleder, May 3, 2024. Our translation.

19   Based on a conversation between Muriel Olesen and the author in 2014 during the Armand Schulthess retrospective at the Dürrenmatt Center in Neuchâtel. Our translation.

20   Lionel Bovier and Christophe Cherix (eds), *L'irrésolution commune d'un engagement équivoque, Ecart, Genève 1969–1982*, MAMCO and Cabinet des Estampes, Geneva, 1997, p. 36. Republished in 2019 with the support of HEAD – Genève. The catalog contains an impressive list of participants: around 50 artists who came to Minkoff and Olesen's kitchen to have their voices recorded.

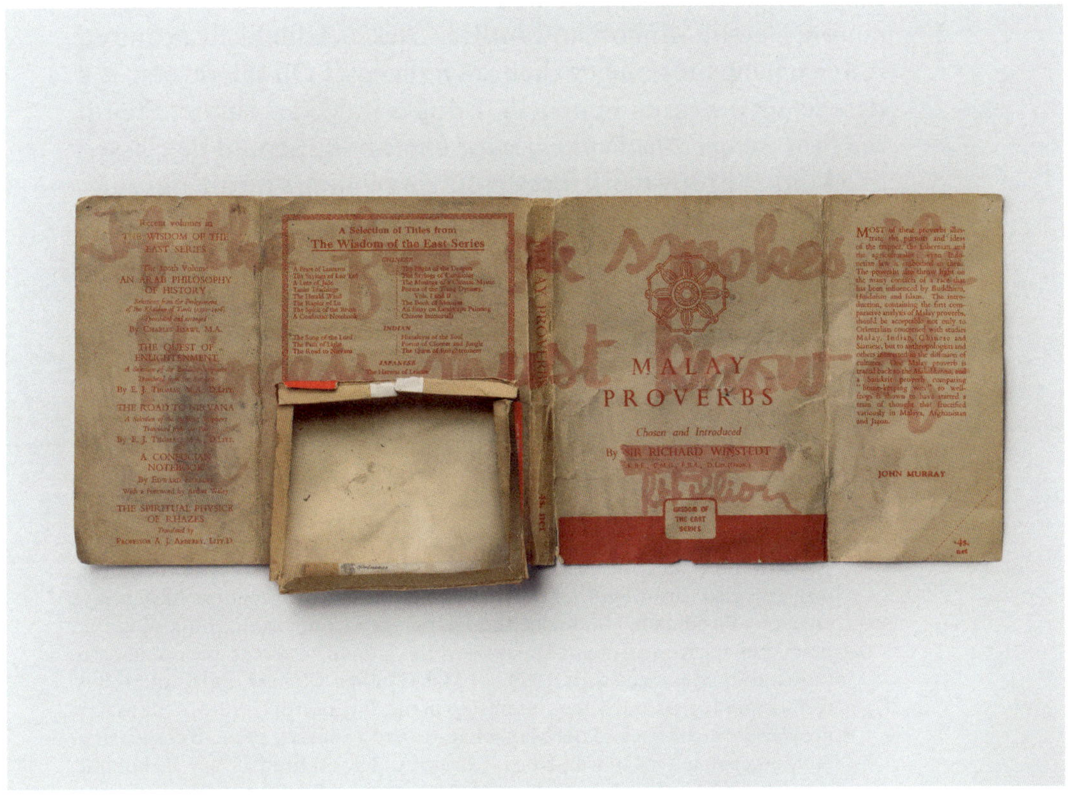

If the Frog Smokes the Princess must know of it, (Malay Proverbs chosen and introduced by… Rt Filliou), c. 1953
book cover, cardboard, plastic, tobacco, felt, 14 × 43.1 × 2 cm
MAMCO collection, bequeathed by Gérald Minkoff and Muriel Olesen

L'Immortelle Mort du Monde/The Deathless Dying of the World (1961) is traditionally considered to be Robert Filliou's first visual work. It was produced around the time that Filliou met Daniel Spoerri, to whom it was dedicated, and marked his entry into the established art circles of the early 1960s. Taking the form of a script for a random play, this collage combines words and colors,[21] foreshadowing the use of text—descriptive, poetic and illustrative texts, as well as ostensible titles—that would go on to be a mainstay of Filliou's oeuvre.

If the Frog Smokes the Princess must know of it… is an enigmatic work. It was bequeathed to MAMCO in 2021 by the artist couple Gérald Minkoff and Muriel Olesen, who likely acquired it in exchange for one of their own pieces.[22] On the reverse is a date (c. 1953) written in pencil. If this is indeed accurate, then *If the Frog Smokes the Princess must know of it…* could be classed as a kind of proto-work foreshadowing Filliou's future output.

This unusual object is "based" on the cover of John Murray's book *Malay Proverbs. Chosen and Introduced by Sir Richard Winstedt.* Published in London in 1950, it is a compendium of over 250 proverbs, sayings, aphorisms, and metaphors that feature heavily in colloquial Malay language. Whereas Cervantes described proverbs as "short sentences drawn from long experience," the following text, penned by the publisher, appears on the book's dust-jacket flap:

> Most of these proverbs illustrate the pursuits and ideas of the trapper, the fisherman and the agriculturalist; even Indonesian law is embodied in them. The proverbs also throw light on the many contacts of a race that has been influenced by Buddhism, Hinduism and Islam. The introduction, containing the first comparative analysis of Malay proverbs, should be acceptable not only to Orientalists concerned with studies of Malay, Indian, Chinese, and Siamese, but to anthropologists and others interested in the diffusion of cultures. One Malay proverb is traced back to the Mahabharata, and a Sanskrit proverb comparing 'home-keeping wits' to well-frogs is shown to have started a train of thought that fructified variously in Malaya, Afghanistan and Japan.

Filliou was undoubtedly drawn to this syncretism—a blend of philosophical thought and popular morality. He crossed out the author's name and replaced it with his own, introducing a proverb of his own invention: "If the frog smokes the princess must know of it." On the dust jacket is glued a box of *Leichte Princess*[23] cigarettes, produced by the German firm Bibertis, with just one cigarette left inside. Tack holes reveal that the object was once affixed to a wall.

As Pierre Tilman wrote in his extensive biography of Filliou, the artist lived seven lives in one.[24] In 1953, after obtaining a master's degree in economics from the University of California, he went to South Korea to work for the United Nations Korean Reconstruction Agency on a five-year reconstruction plan. During his travels in East Asia, he visited Japan and discovered Kabuki theater and Zen Buddhism. Did he smoke *Leichte Princess* cigarettes? In 1944, while in hiding as a member of the Resistance, he rolled his cigarettes with JOB papers.[25] Later, "he smoked beedies tied with pink thread, which made the ends look pretty in the ashtray. Beedies were imported from India. They were not available in France. They were sold by Davidoff in Switzerland. Gérald Minkoff's wife Muriel, who lived in Geneva, sent them to him in Flayosc."[26]

Filliou's watershed moment came in 1953:

> as he stopped keeping company with macroeconomic systems and likely gave up the associated illusion of having some influence over people and events. He embraced life as a wanderer, seeking out a different identity and trying to carve out a new place in the world. Filliou traveled light, fashioning a nomadic lifestyle consisting of bits of string, next to nothing, cardboard boxes, postcards for mass circulation, notes that were half-serious and half-ironic, cheerful manifestos, and bric(k)-a-brac of all kinds. His was an art made on the move, a proliferation of words and symbols where everything was equal, in a system of universal equivalence in which convention was to be eschewed and originality embraced. A system in which the principles of political economy gave way to the principles of poetical economy.[27]

This work bears all the formal and intellectual hallmarks of Filliou's output: it blends text and everyday objects in the form of an ambiguous assemblage so typical of an artist known to be a second-rate do-it-yourselfer. *If the Frog Smokes the Princess must know of it…* is an example of one of Filliou's "mind-openers," crafted with whatever the artist had at hand: a book of proverbs and a box of cigarettes, his sharp mind doing the rest.

21   *"L'Immortelle Mort du Monde/ The Deathless Dying of the World* is a play that serves as a metaphor for chance. The words each actor reads depend on the color of the performer immediately to their right. There are 10 characters dressed in blue, red and green knit sweaters. The colors they wear determine what they say when they meet. It is a play about the arbitrariness of thought." Filliou, R., Dreyfus, C., Gibertie, A. and Noël, A. (1988), *Inter*, (38), 4–15, p. 7: https://www.erudit.org/ fr/revues/inter/1988-n38-inter1104373/ 46975ac/. Our translation.

22   Regrettably, we were unable to obtain any information about how it came into their possession.

23   These cigarettes were produced in Germany, first in Bremen and then in Berlin, by the Brinkmann factory.

24   Pierre Tilman, *Robert Filliou: Nationalité poète*, Les presses du réel, Dijon, 2006, p. 9. Much of the biographical information cited here comes from this book.

25   "Job" was the name Filliou adopted as a combatant during the Second World War. The Job of biblical fame was an important figure throughout his life.

26   Pierre Tilman, *op. cit.*, p. 10. Marika Malacorda also supplied Filliou with beedies. Our translation.

27   Paul-Hervé Parsy, "Je suis le rêve de quel papillon ?" in *Robert Filliou – Poet. Sammlung Feelisch*, exhibition catalog, Galerie der Stadt Remscheid, Remscheid, 1997, p. 111. Our translation.

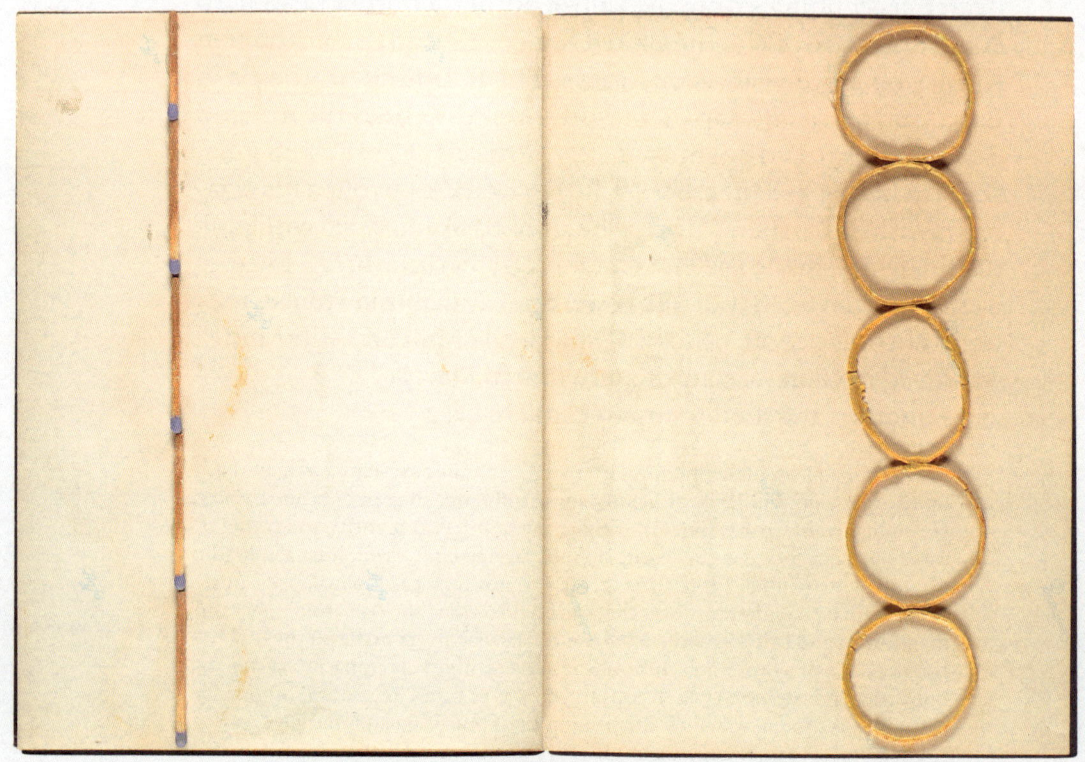

Poï-Poï, 1961
typewritten prints and photomontage (positive and negative), fingerprints, collage of rubber bands and matches on paper
first Filliou exhibition catalog, Copenhagen, Galerie Köpcke, unbound, unpaginated, handmade, each copy unique, 21.2 × 14.7 cm (closed)
MAMCO collection, donated by Marianne Filliou

In June and July 1961, Robert Filliou held his first solo exhibition at the gallery owned by German artist Arthur (Addi) Köpcke[28] in Copenhagen. He was 35 at the time, and his life had already taken many twists and turns: a past as a Resistance fighter and professional poker player, a master's degree in political economy, and a life as a wandering poet in Andalusia. He spoke French, English and German, sometimes using all three languages simultaneously in his writing.

In the five short years it existed (1958–1963), Köpcke's small gallery hosted some of the most remarkable exhibitions held in Denmark at the time. The Filliou show was the first *Poï-Poï*[29] event, and it featured "mummified objects," "poem-objects," and "action poems," including *L'Immortelle Mort du Monde/The Deathless Dying of the World* and *A 53 Kilos Poem*.[30]

A handmade catalog accompanied the exhibition. Produced in an unknown number of unique copies, it is an unassuming object. Inside the cover—a black, A4-sized sheet of drawing paper, folded in half, with no inscriptions—are five blank sheets, also folded in half, and typewritten text with a photomontage (positive on the front, negative on the back), reflecting the association between text and object that would go on to be a mainstay of Filliou's work. The text is the only part of the catalog that was mechanically reproduced. The leaves are not bound. On the blank pages, Filliou glued everyday objects or added fingerprints. Elastic bands, matches and fingerprints span the length or width of each page, as if serving as measuring devices: a single page measures 5 elastic bands, 4¾ matches or 11 fingerprints high. The central double-page, meanwhile, measures 14½ fingerprints across.

With this catalog, Filliou proposed an alternative to the standard, metric system of measurement. He took this approach further in the text inside, suggesting that a person's height could be expressed in tomatoes (he was 60 tomatoes tall) and that his age was equivalent to 111,225 train journeys between Copenhagen and Paris. In inventing substitutes for accepted, standardized scales, he laid the foundations for a broader process of reflection, some aspects of which—the absence of hierarchy and the eschewing of competition—would lead, in 1968, to his "Principle of Equivalence," which postulated that "well made," "badly made," and "not made" were all equivalent. In addition to being playful, inventive and transgressive, these new scales of value were intended to constantly challenge established practices.

After abandoning a mapped-out career as an economist, Filliou got by through bartering, existing in a kind of survival economy where he made the most of whatever he had. By incorporating everyday objects into his poems, he was staying true to the "Principles of Poetical Economy," which advocated for a society in which every person would become an artist. The mummified objects[31] Filliou exhibited in Copenhagen were not for sale, but he was open to bartering them for the essential items he and his partner[32] needed—a mattress, a bed, or a table. At the end of the exhibition, Spoerri bought the entire contents of the couple's room—furniture and objects alike—and turned them into 10 "snare-pictures."[33] In this way, objects passed from hand to hand and were recycled in unexpected ways and renewed. In a note scribbled on a piece of paper for a friend, Filliou wrote: "Art as a new source of energy."

This text was written for the *Uniques* exhibition catalog, Fondation Bodmer, Flammarion, Paris, 2018, p. 90–93. The notes relating to Galerie Köpcke have been added.

28   "Originally from Hamburg, Addi Köpcke still wore his grease-stained Prince Henry cap, even though he had been living in Copenhagen for many years with his wife: a sturdy woman with a stocky frame who had to drag the gaunt, inveterate beer-drinker home after every session. The Danes should erect a monument to him, for it was he who brought the art of the 1960s to Copenhagen and showed them what it was all about." Daniel Spoerri, "Addi Koepcke et sa galerie," in *Restaurant Spoerri*, exhibition catalog, Jeu de Paume, Paris, 2002, p. 33. Our translation.

29   The term *Poï-Poï* refers to a ritualistic, rhythmical style of speech employed by the Dogon people of Mali.

30   *Poï-Poï Riddersalen (A 53 Kilos Poem)* was a performance in which 53 kilograms of gravel were transferred from Filliou's suitcase to Köpcke's, with the performer reciting *Poï-Poï* each time. The performance ended when the contents of one suitcase had been completely moved to the other.

31   "Note on *Momified* and Measured Objects: Perhaps talking, certainly recording one's words on tape, creating, making durable, making one's own, employing the possessive—all these things imply *momifying* an object, a thing, an emotion, intuition, idea... (Here is a chair. Van Gogh paints it. In a sense, he *momifies* it. Spoerri uses it in a snare-picture. In a sense, he *momifies* it.) *De-momifying* what others— or yourself—have done also is creating.... Others, time, death are great *de-momificators*. I have wanted to see what the result would be if I *momified* directly some objects, with strings, elastic, thread, rope... Whatever happened to be within easy reach at the time. POIPOI." Filliou's typewritten note on mummified objects in his 1961 catalog, quoted in Daniel Spoerri *et al.*, *An Anecdoted Topography of Chance*, Something Else Press, New York, 1966, p. 44.

32   Filliou met Marianne Staffeldt, a Danish high-school student, in 1957. Their daughter Marcelline was born in Copenhagen in 1961.

33   Daniel Spoerri: "I was in Denmark to help organize the 'Art in Motion' (Bevaegelse I Kunsten) exhibition. Since the museum decided it could get along without my assistance, I took advantage of the opportunity that Addi Koepcke gave me to have a show in his gallery. Fate willed that I live at Robert Filliou's, who, since he had been ordered to leave the country, gave up his apartment and let me 'snare' everything I could find there: altogether ten pictures." *An Anecdoted Topography of Chance*, op. cit., p. 15.

LA FÊTE À LA GIOCONDE SOUS LE HAUT PATRONAGE DE SA TRASCENDENCE G.M.O.G.G. MARCEL DUCHAMP (JOCONDOLOGUE)

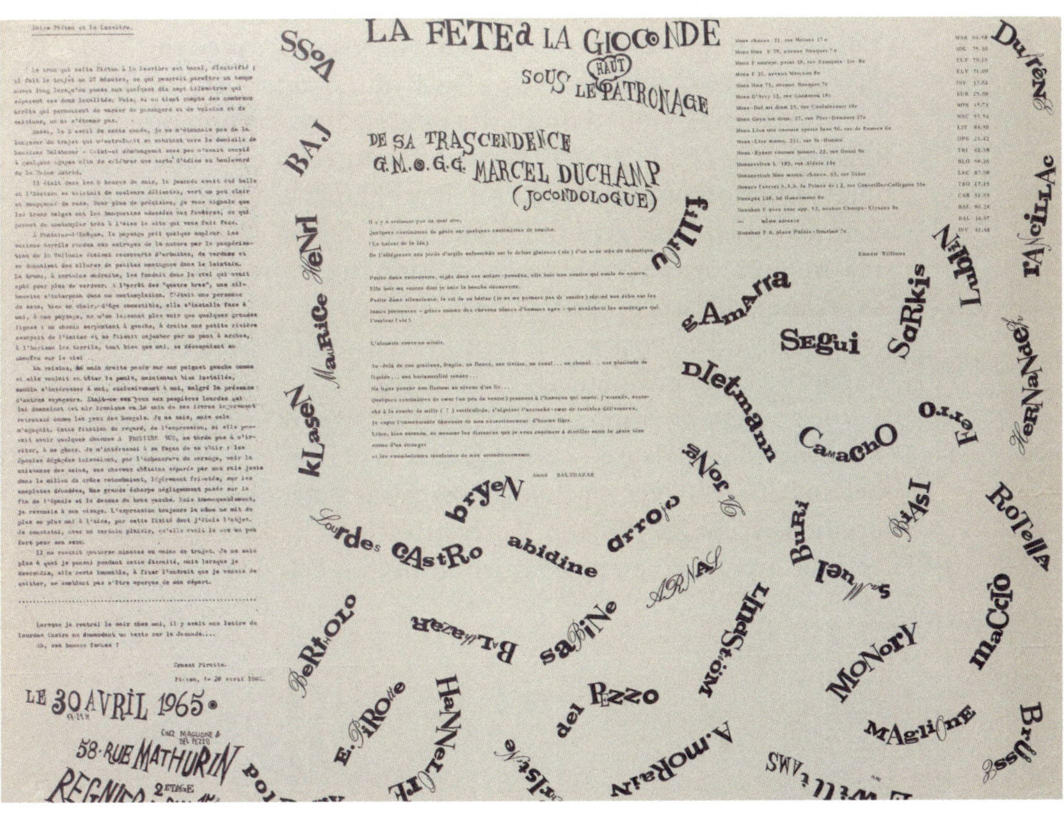

La Fête à la Gioconde sous le haut patronage de sa trascendence G.M.O.G.G. Marcel Duchamp (Jocondologue), collective work, 1965
offset lithograph, 50 × 66 cm
MAMCO collection

In April 1965, around 40 artists[34] gathered at Milvia Maglione and Lucio del Pezzo's home, at 58 Rue Mathurin-Régnier in the 15th arrondissement of Paris, to mark *La Fête à la Gioconde* (The Celebration of the Mona Lisa), under the "high patronage of the most famous of *Jocondologues*," Marcel Duchamp.[35] The event was attended by a motley assortment of poets, pataphysicists, New

Realists, Situationists, New Figurationists, members of the Salon de la Jeune Peinture, and followers of the Fluxus movement. In the 1960s, Paris was a hotbed of cross-fertilization with galleries, artists and magazines acting as intermediaries, bringing people and ideas together. The artists who gathered for this celebration came prepared to do battle over what Huysmans called the "submarine goddess," foreshadowing Duchamp's iconoclastic practice.

This poster, signed by all the participants, commemorated this opening act: each artist brought along their own, irreverent interpretation of the *Mona Lisa*. For Filliou's contribution, the famous subject was removed from her armchair (and her pedestal) and became a janitor, busy cleaning the stairs [FIG. 13]. Four years later, this work, entitled *La Joconde est dans les escaliers / Bin in zehn Minuten zurück*, was reproduced and released in several copies by Edition Tangente, Heidelberg.

On 20 October 1965, several months after the original event, a second—less private—celebration was held at Galerie Mathias Fels in Paris. The accompanying poster was almost identical to the original except for the title, Duchamp's name had been removed, and the artists were merely celebrating *"La Fête à la Joconde."*

34   According to the poster, the following were present: Abidine, Arnal, Arroyo, Baj, Balthazar, Bertholo, Biasi, Bryen, Brüsse, Bury, Camacho, Christen, de Jong, del Pezzo, Dietman, Dufrêne, Gamarra, Ferro, Filliou, Hannelore, Maurice Henri, Hernandez, Klasen, Lindström, Lourdes Castro, Lubin, Maccló, Maglione, A. Morain, Monory, E. Pirotte, Rancillac, Rotella, Sabine, Sarkis, Segui, Voss and E. Williams.

35   "At the time, Duchamp was just like the rest of us: there was no hierarchy," recalls Sarkis, who created a camouflage portrait of the *Mona Lisa* for the occasion (conversation with the author, April 2, 2024). Our translation.

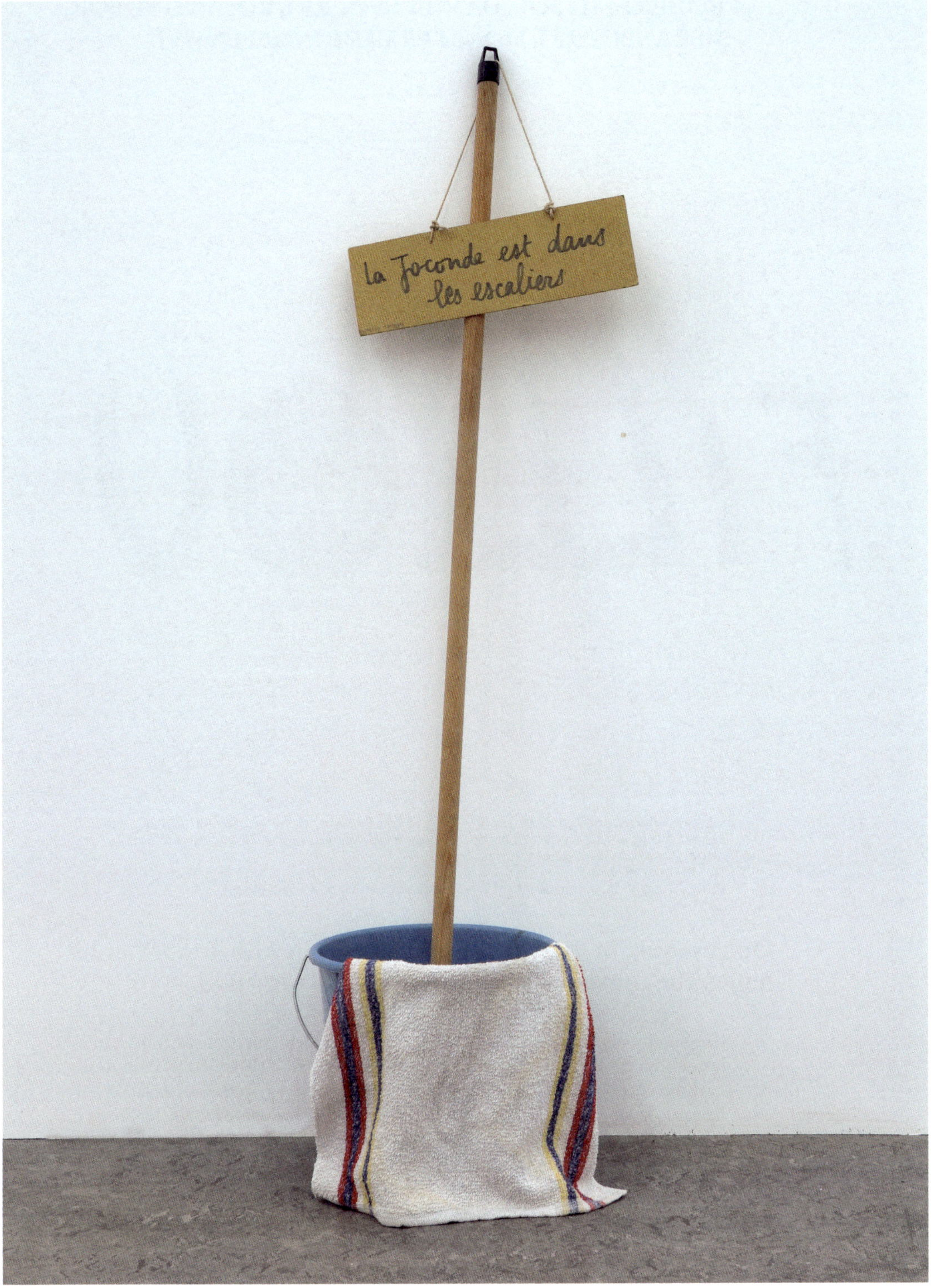

[FIG.13] *La Joconde est dans les escaliers / Bin in zehn Minuten zurück. Mona Lisa,* 1969
Coll. FRAC Champagne-Ardenne, Reims

ROBERT FILLIOU, DANIEL SPOERRI, ROLAND TOPOR, VERA SPOERRI, *MONSTERS ARE INOFFENSIVE*

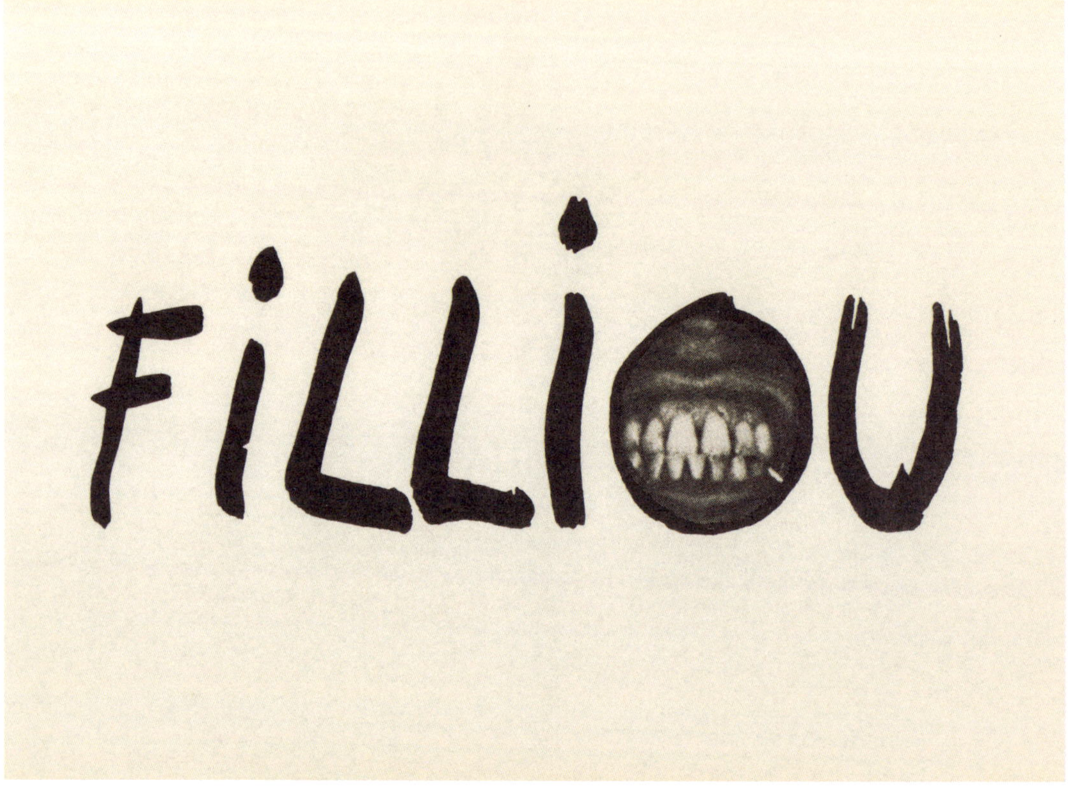

Robert Filliou, Daniel Spoerri, Roland Topor, Vera Spoerri, *Monsters Are Inoffensive*, 1967
set of 22 black-and-white printed postcards inside an envelope, Fluxus, Division of
Implosions Inc., George Maciunas, New York
11 × 16 cm (per item)
MAMCO collection, bequeathed by Gérald Minkoff and Muriel Olesen

One evening in May 1966, Spoerri met up with Topor[36] at his home. The conversation between the two turned to:

the paucity of possibilities of the human body, with its single head, four extremities and narrowly distributed erogenous zones, often shriveled by complexes, or miraculously displaced in monsters; in the perverse, in the depraved, where this toe, that earlobe or even external objects replace and expand the limits of

SPOERRI

TOPOR

nature in a way that is almost enviable (and I could not help but think of my much-admired neighbor on Rue Mouffetard, Hans Bellmer, whose drawings are imbued with this same concern for substitution and expansion). We had another six or seven impromptu sessions like these, arranged according to our free time and guided by our ideas at the time. Those hours spent talking and laughing remain my fondest memory. Robert Filliou later joined us while he was visiting Paris, coming up with titles for the photos in his own distinctive way.[37]

The project was originally intended to be a book, but no French publisher could be persuaded to take it on. In the end, George Maciunas, based in New York, suggested publishing a series of postcards instead. Topor produced the drawings, Filliou and Daniel Spoerri worked on the photographs and collages, and Vera Spoerri took photos of the end result. The reverse of each postcard features a "caption" penned by Filliou.[38] These cards, like much Fluxus output, were originally encased in a plastic box. This was later replaced with an envelope. Three of the 22 postcards bear the artists' names along with a "portrait photo" of each contributor—a detail of their face or a portion of their body enclosed within the letter "O" in their surname. Some images are pierced with holes into which fingers are inserted, producing an even more grotesque effect. Others feature cutouts from magazines or are black-and-white photographs—of heads, torsos, feet, and other anatomical details—along with hastily executed drawings by Topor.

Maciunas would later recycle the idea and the title for a series of prototype tablecloths and table tops—produced in collaboration with Filliou, Spoerri, Peter Moore, and Roberts Watts—with "fragments of the human body, sometimes identifiable as the forearms or torsos of dinner guests...."[39]

36   Topor, like Filliou, was introduced to avant-garde art circles by Spoerri. "Daniel [Spoerri] revealed to me the existence of a new avant-garde movement whose members claimed to be followers of Duchamp and Cage. It was a real joy for me to learn that there were not only the Lyrical Abstractionists like [Georges] Mathieu, the Social Realists, the Tachists, the School of Paris, and the Lettrists, but also, just about everywhere in the world, high-quality artists following a tradition closer to Dada and black humor, insolently blending derision and nonsense. I felt as if I'd finally found my tribe. Through Daniel, I met Robert Filliou, Erik Dietman, Dieter Roth, Kudo and George Brecht." Alexandre Devaux, *Topor et les enjeux de l'art contemporain*, Éditions de la Sorbonne, Paris, 2017, note 16: www.cairn.info/revue-sociétés-et-représentations-2017-2-page-89.htm. Our translation.

37   "Monsters are inoffensive," facsimile of the original edition, plus Daniel Spoerri's letter to the publishers, the *"les monstres sont inoffensifs"* ("monsters are inoffensive") text written by Roland Topor, and three photographs by Vera Spoerri, Galerie Anne Barrault, Paris, 2017.

38   Sylvie Jouval, *Robert Filliou: éditions & multiples*, Les presses du réel, Dijon, 2003, p. 29.

39   Sylvie Jouval, *op. cit.*, p. 31. Our translation.

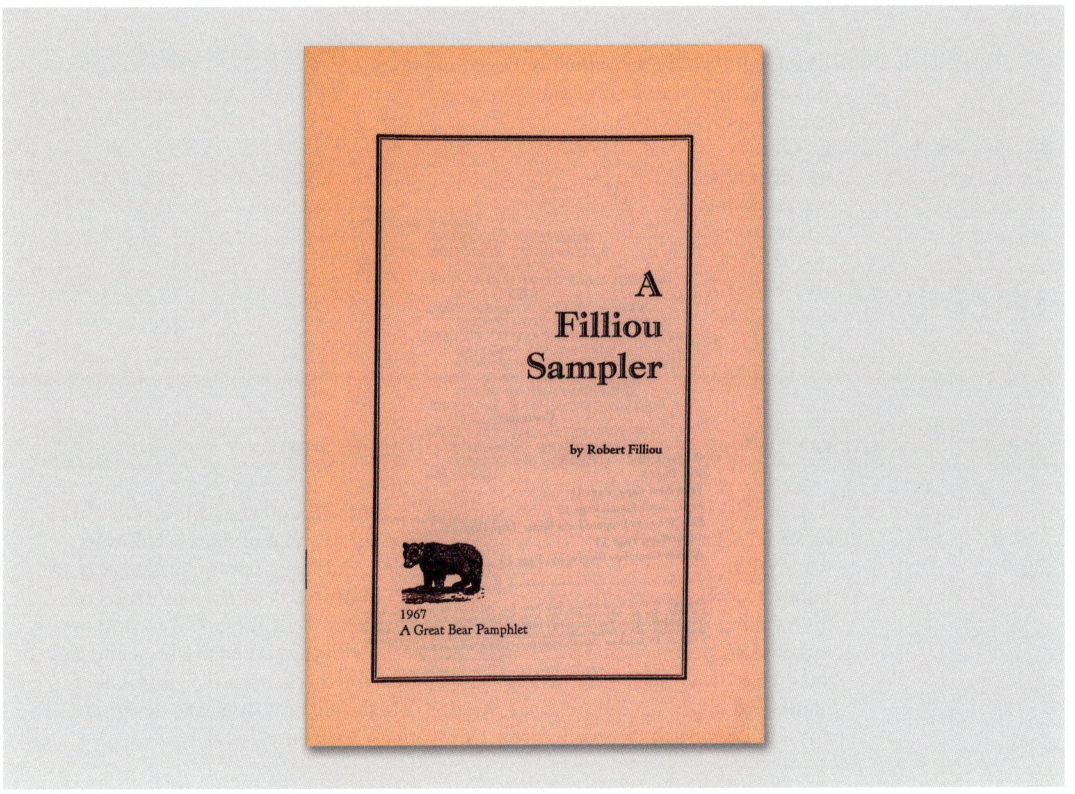

A Filliou Sampler, 1967
pamphlet [16 p.], text in English, black-and-white print, Something Else Press, New York
22 × 14 cm
MAMCO collection, bequeathed by Gérald Minkoff and Muriel Olesen

This work was part of the *A Great Bear Pamphlet* series conceived by Dick Higgins, the founder of Something Else Press. This publication, one of 20 in the series released between 1965 and 1967, features poems written by Filliou between 1958 and 1964.

Yes. An action poem paints a portrait of the adult male poet, starting with his physical characteristics (height, skeleton, limbs), then moving on to his diet and digestion, his reproductive organs, his sensitivity and his senses, before concluding with his intelligence and his articulate speech—that which "distinguishes him most from animals." In part two, Filliou offers up a kind of self-portrait:

> *LE FILLIOU IDEAL (written in Paris in 1964)*
> It is an action poem, and I am
> going to perform it.
> Its score is:
> not deciding
> not choosing
> not wanting
> not owning
> aware of self
> wide awake
> SITTING QUIETLY,
> DOING NOTHING

The poem was accompanied by a publisher's note:

> This work was conceived for performance, and was done at the Cafe au Go-Go in New York, on February 8th, 1965, the first part was read by Alison Knowles, while Filliou sat cross-legged upstage, motionless and silent. For the second part, Filliou stood up, spoke the words which we have printed here, then returned to his former position. Philip Corner improvised an almost silent musical accompaniment. The performance continued until all those in the audience who seemed anxious to leave had done so. It should be noted also, that the title given here names Filliou as "Le Filliou Ideal," but this title should be changed to designate any adult male poet who performs this work as "Le (name) Ideal."

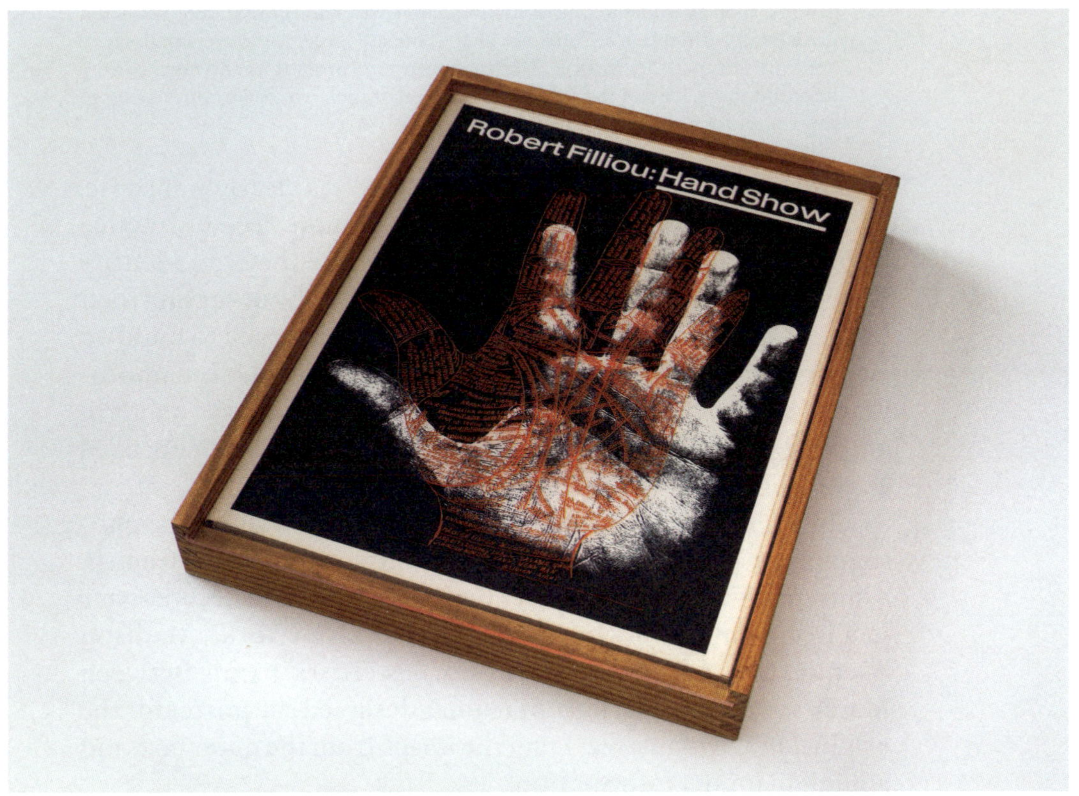

Hand Show, 1967, case with sliding Plexiglas lid, silkscreen-printed in red, containing 24 black-and-white silkscreen prints representing the hands of Arman, Ay-O, Robert Breer, Mark Brusse, Pol Bury, John Cage, Christo, Red Grooms, Robert Filliou, Dick Higgins, Scott Hyde, Alain Jacquet, Jasper Johns, Ray Johnson, Alison Knowles, Roy Lichtenstein, Jackson Mac Low, Marisol, Claes Oldenburg, Benjamin Patterson, Takis, Andy Warhol, Robert Watts, and Emmett Williams, plus a presentation leaflet. Photographs by Scott Hyde SABA-Studio, No. 71/150, 4.2 × 30 × 24.2 cm
MAMCO collection

This publication draws on the principles of palmistry, a pseudo-scientific divinatory practice that remains popular to this day. Just as palmist Josef Ranald analyzed the handprints of Franklin D. Roosevelt, Benito Mussolini and Adolf Hitler in his 1938 book *How to Know People by their Hands*, so here, Filliou applied the same technique to artists' hands in an attempt to unlock the "key to art":

I had the idea that the key to art could be found by studying the meaning or significance of every part of artists' hands, every line, every sign, every shape. As a group, artists share many characteristics that set them apart from other groups (such as soldiers). But if you look at artists' hands separately, you soon notice huge differences. You'll see that some are large, some are small, some are firm and some are flexible. With cautious interpretations and clues dotted here and there, we can form our own opinion of their works without having to rely on critics as intermediaries…[40]

This text, which takes a swipe at art critics, is clearly nonsense. Palmistry has much in common with the more recent practice of physiognomy, exponents of which believe they can identify things about a person's character or personality by observing their physical appearance. The technique was notably used to build up a typical "profile" of the most dangerous criminals. The photographs for *Hand Show* were made by coating the artists' hands in graphite or another black material, much like the black ink used by the police to take fingerprints.

In addition to publishing the book, Filliou wanted the photographs to go on display—but in a public location rather than in a museum. With Andy Warhol's help, he managed to secure space in a front window at the Tiffany store on New York's Madison Avenue, where he exhibited five of his artists' hands between March 27 and April 12, 1967. Maciunas designed the poster for the exhibition at Tiffany, recycling the image from the outer box, and adding mapping information.

40   Sylvie Jouval, *op. cit.*, p. 35.
Our translation.

POÈME COLLECTIF

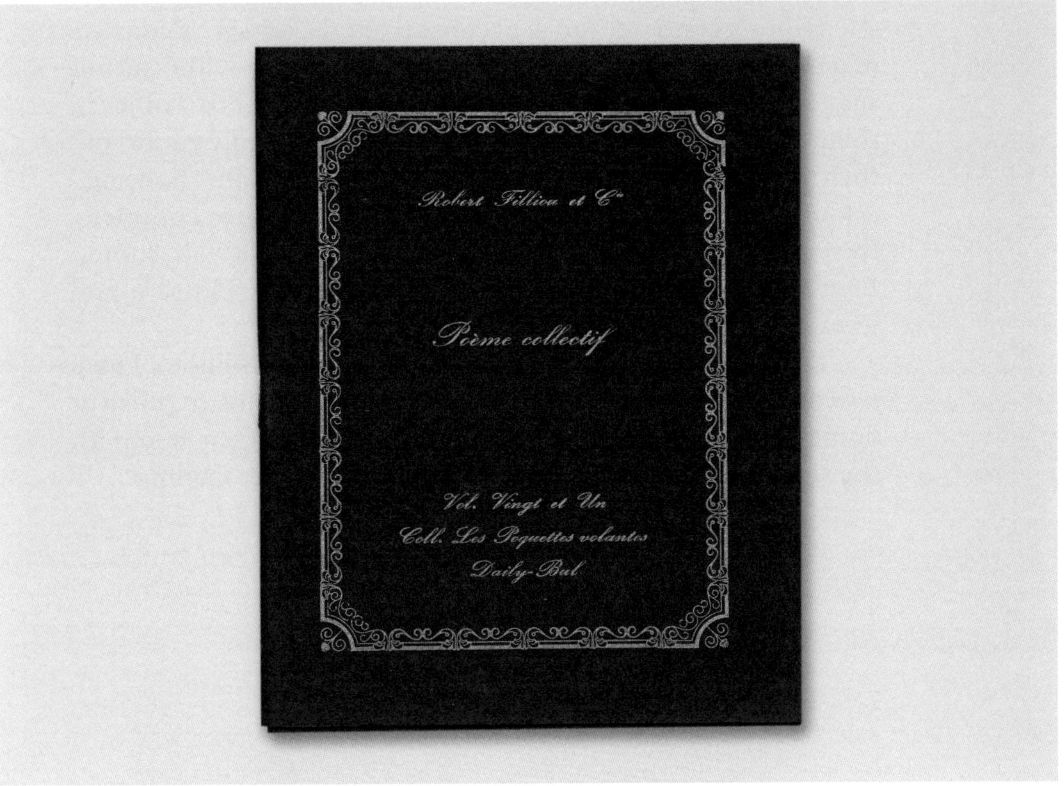

Poème collectif, 1968
artist's book, [24 p.] and insert, Daily-Bul, La Louvière
1,000 copies, numbered starting from No. 96
13.6 × 11 cm
MAMCO collection, bequeathed by Gérald Minkoff and Muriel Olesen

In the 1960s and 1970s, the publisher and poet André Balthazar served as the director of the Center for Engravings and the Printed Image in La Louvière and ran the Daily-Bul publishing house, the latter of which he co-founded with the sculptor Pol Bury. Between 1965 and 1979, they released *Les Poquettes volantes*, a series of small volumes of texts and drawings printed on A4 paper and folded into four so they could easily be slipped into an envelope. With a print run of a thousand copies, these short publications were described as "tasty *zakuskis* of the avant-garde." *Poème collectif* was the 21st issue in the series.

Filliou's contribution is peculiar from the outset: it consists of a set of instructions followed by 16 blank pages. The author suggests writing on the first page "the names of 5 to 7 objects, things, emotions, feelings, etc. that you would gladly get rid of," then having the other pages filled by "15 people of your choosing." A loose leaf hides the previous contributions. Once complete, the collective poem—signed "Robert Filliou & Cie"—becomes: *Epaves de l'Homme – poème de sa nature morte* (Flotsam and Jetsam of Humanity – still life poem).

Poème collectif draws on similar principles to Filliou's *Longs poèmes courts à terminer chez soi* (Long short poems to finish at home), a series of postcards produced in Copenhagen in 1961 for the sender or recipient to complete before or after mailing.

GALERIE LÉGITIME

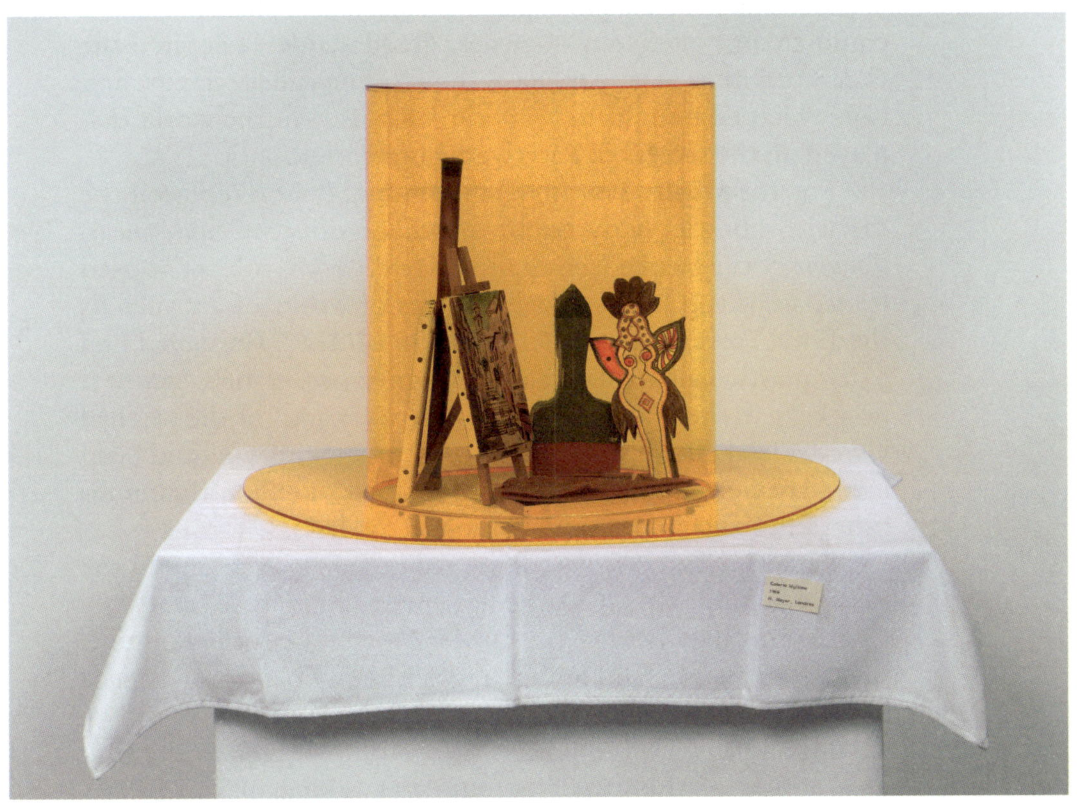

Galerie Légitime, 1966–1968
Plexiglas hat, velvet fabric, wood, ink stamp, various artists' works
48 × 68 × 62 cm
Birgit & Ulf Bischoff Collection, on long-term loan to MAMCO

Robert Filliou's *Galerie Légitime*—or at least its 1968 "sculptural" incarnation—is an example of an artist's museum, in the same vein as Marcel Duchamp's *La Boîte-en-Valise*, Marcel Broodthaers' *Musée d'Art Moderne, Département des Aigles*, and Martin Kippenberger's *MOMAS Projekt*. Each of these works takes the form of an imagined (or perhaps "imaginary"[41]) museum whose aim, among other things, is to offer an alternative mode of presentation—one freed from the shackles of conventional galleries and museums.

Filliou had the idea of creating his own exhibition space: he transformed his cap into the *Galerie Légitime*, removing it at the request of passersby to reveal photographs, objects and phrases—which could change every day—sewn or glued inside. "I created the *Galerie Légitime* in January 1962. The very first gallery was my first cap, which I'd bought 10 years earlier in Tokyo. The works displayed on the streets of Paris were my creation."

For *The Misfits' Fair* (1962) in London, Filliou replaced the cap with a bowler hat. And for *Galerie Légitime – Couvre chef(s) d'oeuvre(s)*, the head covering took on a different role, as he used transparent top hats to cover images of works of art such as the Eiffel Tower and the Dôme des Invalides. "[I]n 1968, I had 6 or 7 plastic hats made, baptized them also *Galerie Légitime* (I now keep in the one of them I still have versions of the original *Galeries* [sic] *Légitime*)."[42] The artist Ann Noël,[43] who had been invited to Germany by Hansjörg Mayer, one of Filliou's first publishers, helped him make the Plexiglas top hats.

Each *Galerie Légitime* completed in 1968 is different. In the version held by MAMCO, the hat covers "miniature" works by George Brecht, Claude Gilli, Olivier Mosset, Dorothy Iannone, Ay-O, Dan Fischer, and Filliou himself. The whole sits on a piece of white velvet, which is signed and stamped.

Monographs on Filliou's work routinely refer to the first incarnation of the *Galerie Légitime* as taking place in Paris on July 3, 1962, when he presented a "traveling" exhibition by Benjamin Patterson. The two artists walked the streets of Paris from morning to night, from Les Halles to the La Coupole restaurant, following an "approximate" route and schedule which were reproduced on the invitation card designed by George Maciunas. The route included a scheduled stop at 9 a.m. by Gertrude Stein's grave at Père-Lachaise cemetery, and another at 4:30 p.m. in front of the *Mona Lisa* at the Louvre.[44] Filliou and Patterson also paid a visit to Iris Clert's gallery, stopped in front of Paris City Hall to request permission to hold the exhibition, ate at Le Chien qui Tousse, and drank at Les Deux Magots and Le Café de Flore, before finishing at La Coupole. The schedule also included "happenings," "environments," poetry readings, dance performances, and compositions by members of the Fluxus movement (Brecht, Cage, Higgins, Kaprow, and Maciunas).

However, in *An Anecdoted Topography of Chance*, Daniel Spoerri reveals the existence of an earlier project (1961), in the form of a contract: "The idea was born during a tumultuous evening at the sumptuous seaside villa of Aagard Andersen near Helsingør… [Filliou] got the idea of starting a wheelbarrow gallery in Paris, where he was returning soon because of his expulsion from Denmark. Everybody present—Tinguely, Niki de St.-Phalle, Addi and Tut Koepcke, the Andersens, the Halling Kochs, the Ussings, and I—was bowled over by the idea and, convulsed with laughter, made preposterous suggestions, which Filliou took seriously. And to prove to us that he was serious, the following day he sent Tinguely this letter:

Dear Tinguely,

Pursuant to our conversation of last evening, I confirm that the *vernissage* of The Legitimate Gallery will take place during the month of October (or as soon as possible) with an exhibition of your work. The Legitimate Gallery is itinerant. It consists of a wheelbarrow or pushcart, according to need. It travels (legitimately) through the streets, in the highest creative tradition. Upon receipt of your works, I promise to maintain them in good condition, respect your prices, and to follow an itinerary to be worked out with you. My commission will consist of the usual 33 per cent. On your part, you will contribute to the launching of the gallery by sending out invitations to your exhibition, and taking care of publicity (press, television, collectors). The Legitimate Gallery will open as soon as legal formalities are arranged. If the price of the license surpasses my means, you will be expected to advance me the money, to be deducted from my commission. In exchange for your assistance in launching the gallery, I promise to exhibit your "legitimate works" whenever you express the desire, in Paris as well as in the provinces and abroad (I intend to take the gallery to such cities as Brasilia, Tokyo, New York, Moscow, Peking, etc.), respecting, of course, contracts with other artists (Niki de St.-Phalle and Daniel Spoerri have already given their consent). Your confirmation of receipt of this letter will serve as our bond of agreement.

So long,
R. Filliou[45]

The "legitimate gallery" concept spawned a whole series of exhibitions and events, including *The Misfits' Fair*. For Filliou, the term "legitimate" was linked to the problems faced by artists: "I considered it legitimate that art should descend from its heights and onto the streets. And given the disastrous lot of the artist in a society that consigns him to misery, or to prostitution, I considered that anything he could do well (or badly) to earn money was legitimate."[46]

41   Malraux's essay *Le Musée imaginaire* ("The Imaginary Museum," or *Museum without Walls* in its English translation)—a museum that makes up for the shortcomings of human memory—has served as a source of inspiration for many artists. "To all those works of art that it elects, the Museum without Walls provides, if not the eternity sought by the sculptors of Sumer or Babylon, nor the immortality sought by Phidias and Michelangelo, at least an enigmatic deliverance from time. And if it leads to a Louvre that is crowded rather than deserted, it is because the true museum is the presence, in life, of that which ought to belong to death." André Malraux, *Le Musée imaginaire*, Folio, Paris, 1996. Our translation.

42   Excerpt from a letter sent by Robert Filliou to Peggy Gale in September 1982, published in *Museum by Artists*, edited by AA Bronson & Peggy Gale, Art Metropole, Toronto, 1983, p. 90.

43   She went on to work as Dick Higgins' assistant at Something Else Press, where she met Emmett Williams, whom she would later marry.

44   According to Patterson's contribution to the introduction to *Ample Food for Stupid Thought* (1965).

45   Daniel Spoerri *et al.*, *An Anecdoted Topography of Chance*, *op. cit.*, pp. 146–147.

46   *Robert Fillliou* [sic], Centre Pompidou, *op. cit.*, pp. 37–38. Our translation.

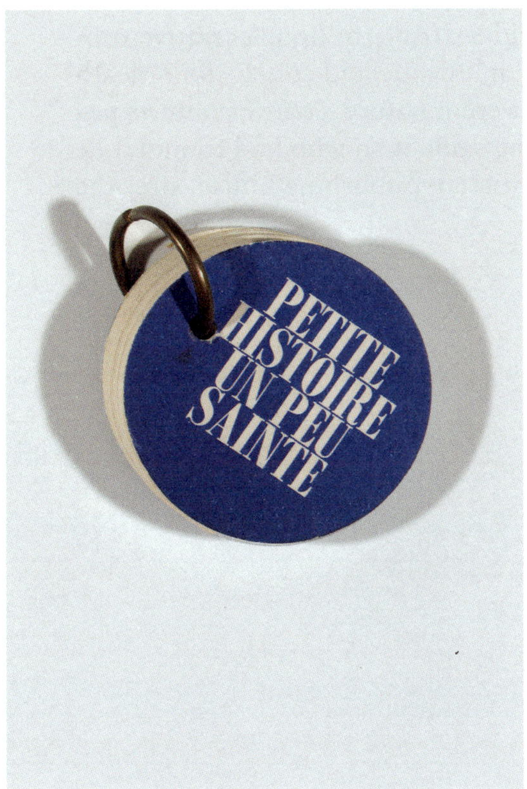

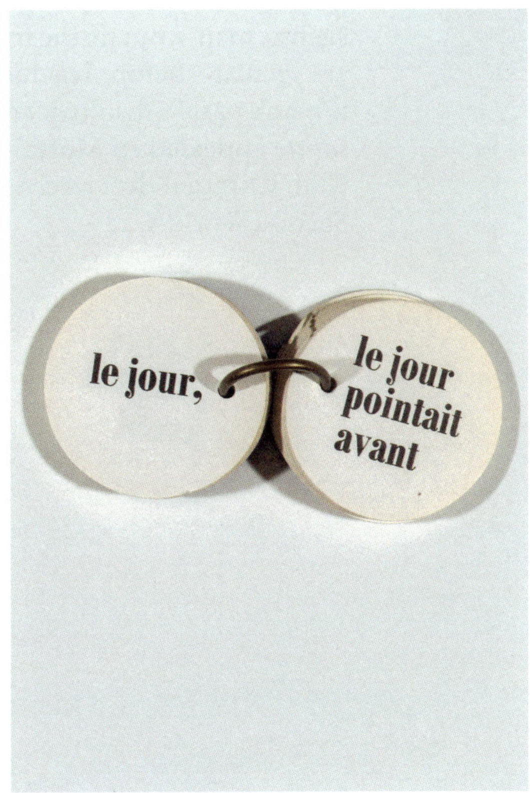

Petite histoire un peu sainte, 1969
circular book bound with brass ring, [100 p.], Robert Morel, Forcalquier, 500 copies; diam.: 6 cm
MAMCO collection, bequeathed by Gérald Minkoff and Muriel Olesen

Robert Filliou chose neither the shape nor the format of this book, which was released as No. 58 in the *O* collection: a series of circular works held together by a brass ring that made their publisher, Robert Morel (1922–1990), famous.

The publishing house's catalog praises the book as "a short text that makes good use of the rhythm of the 'O.' A whole series of different things that worked in a 'before' that is only revealed in the final pages." *Petite histoire un peu sainte* is, in fact, a story

Sophie Costes

about humanity's past: the word *"avant"* (before) recurs like a leitmotif in the succession of short sentences that make up this prose poem. It touches on a vast array of themes—some biblical, such as man, woman, the forbidden fruit, the flood narrative, others secular—before reaching an unexpected conclusion: "death is man's past." Despite its irreverent nature, *Petite histoire un peu sainte* appealed to Morel—the same man who had founded Le Club Chrétien du Livre, a Christian publishing house, after the Second World War.

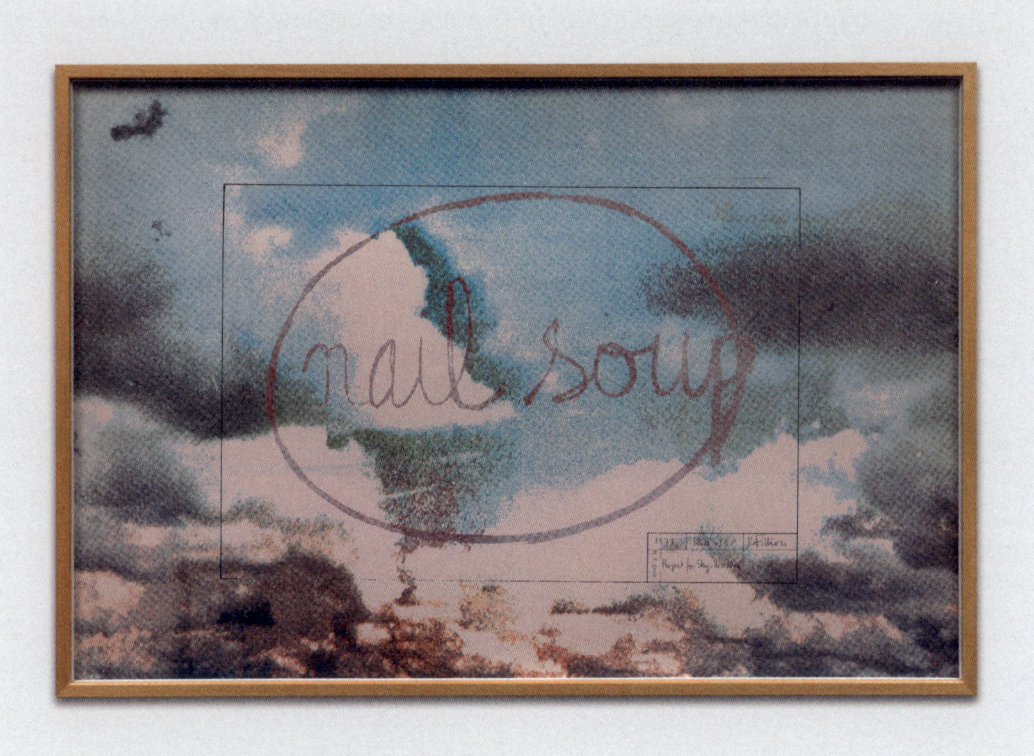

Project for Sky-Writing (Nail Soup), Planche 5, 1971
silkscreen print; 62.5 × 95 cm (including frame)
Hartmut Kaminski, Düsseldorf, A.P.
MAMCO collection, bequeathed by Gérald Minkoff and Muriel Olesen

This plate is part of a portfolio of 10 silkscreen prints. Of the 10 copies that were originally produced, five were taken apart so that the plates could be distributed separately. Like *7 Childlike Uses of Warlike Material* (1971) and *Research in Arts and Astrology* (1972), these plates were published by Hartmut Kaminski in Düsseldorf.

Over each skyscape is superimposed a short piece of text contained within a rectangle, almost like a haiku. The enigmatic quality of these compositions prompts us to reflect on their meaning, causing us to feel an almost childlike wonder as we imagine these ephemeral poems being written across the sky in vaporous letters in an airplane's wake—which is exactly what happened five years later in the skies over New York:

> 'Projects for Sky-Writing'. It's ten screenprints. The plan was to have a plane write it in the sky. And that has actually been done since. By Charlotte Moorman— it could only be her—at Free Speech Festival [in New York in 1976]. Someone, perhaps someone in Germany, told me he got back from New York and had seen 'LOVE = UFO' in the sky.

Several years later, on February 27, 1983, Filliou wrote a letter addressed to "Dear Skywatcher." On the back of the envelope, he proposed a model for a new sky-writing project: "art is what makes life more interesting than art." Here, Filliou cast this oft-quoted phrase as a "statement" inscribed in the skies above our heads.

On July 1, 2016, as part of the celebrations for art's 1,000,053[rd] birthday, MAMCO commissioned a specially trained pilot to sky-write a few short Filliou poems above Geneva.

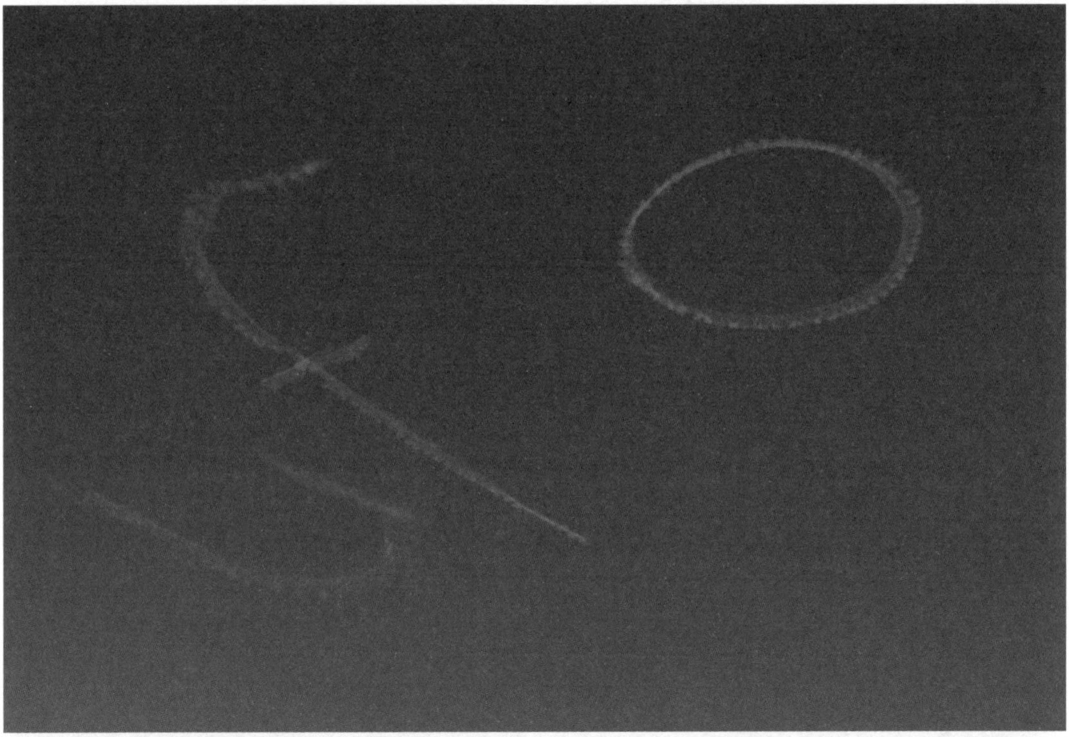

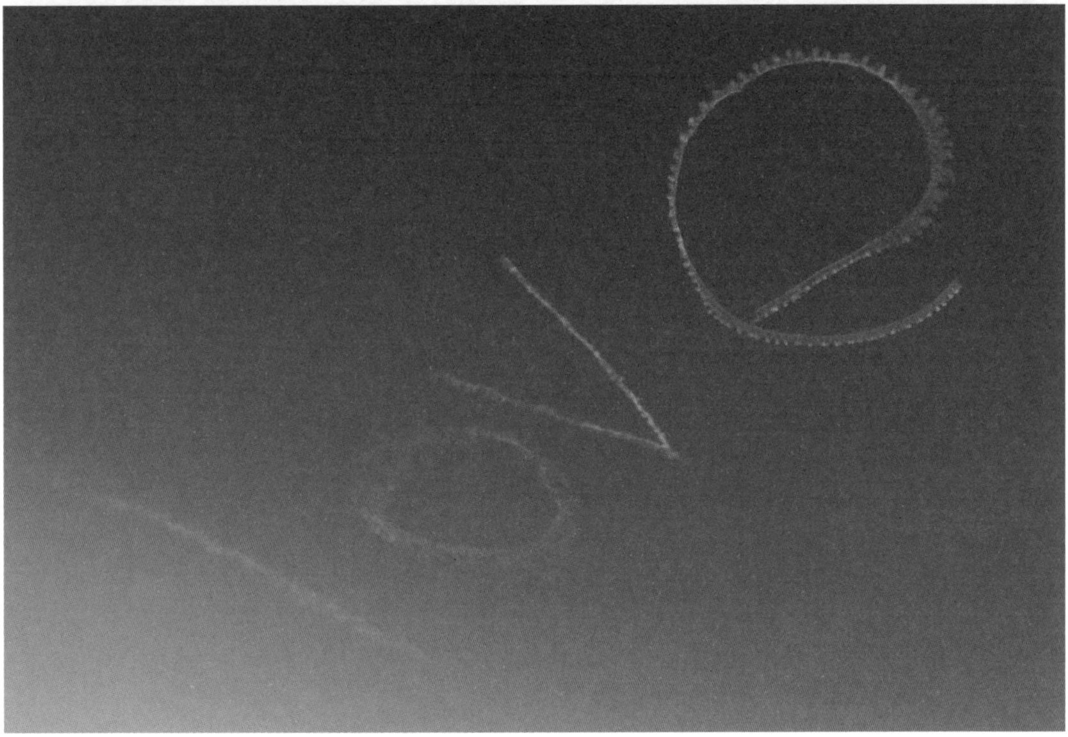

Sky-Writing above Lake Geneva, 2016

7 CHILDLIKE USES OF WARLIKE MATERIAL

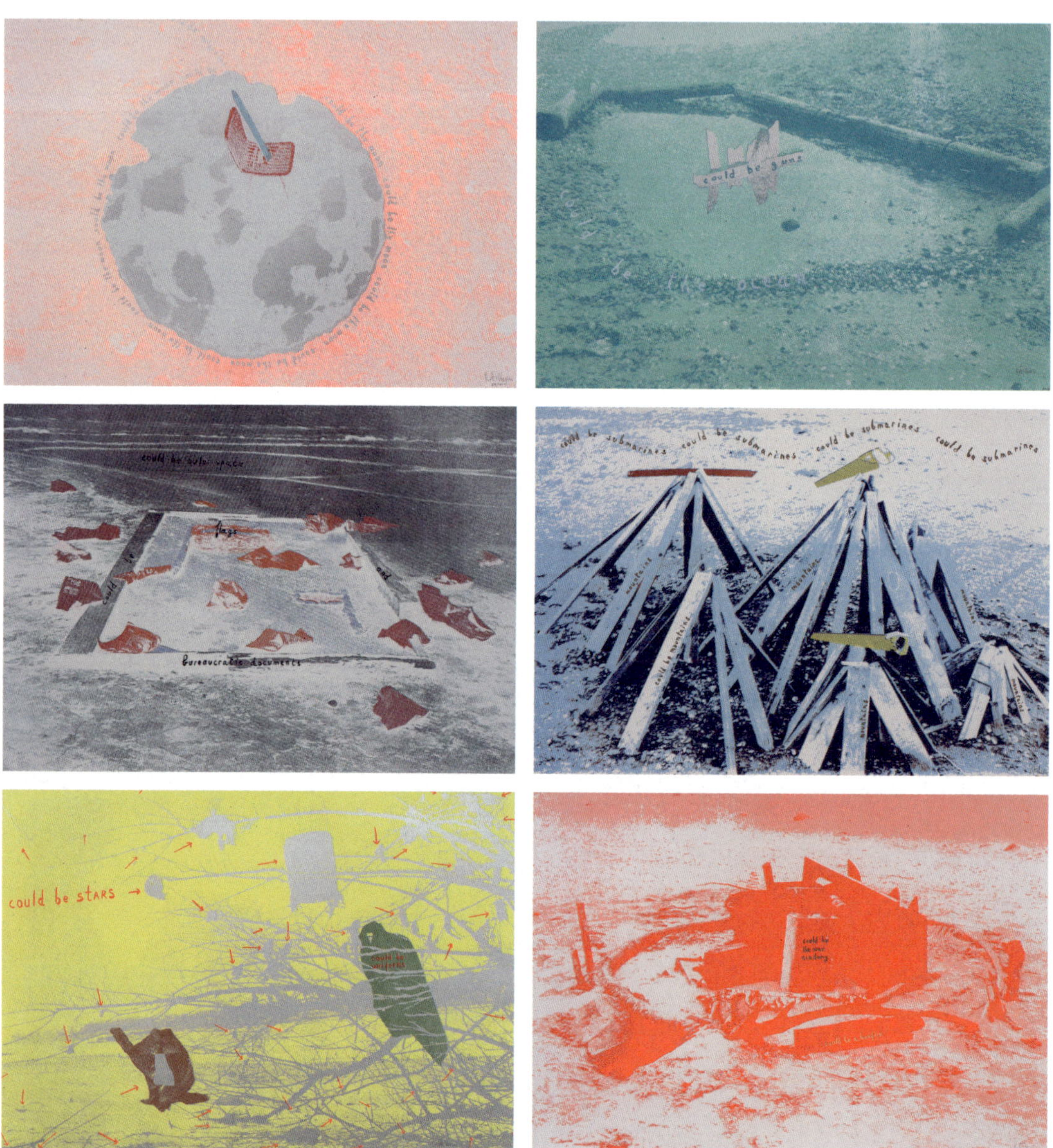

7 Childlike Uses of Warlike Material, 1971
portfolio of seven silkscreen prints in a silkscreen-printed cardboard folder
52 × 72 cm (per item including frame)
Hartmut Kaminski, Düsseldorf, 100 copies
MAMCO collection

Robert Filliou

Children have more sophisticated imaginations than adults because theirs have yet to be constrained by rigid systems of thinking. In his works, Filliou often emphasized the connecting power of play—a practice that is typically associated with children and, in some societies, is seen as a serious tool for learning.

While living in Germany, during one of his walks along the banks of the Rhine, Filliou noticed various objects caught on the branches by the wind or carried by the river and deposited on the silt. These scattered items were photographed by Harmut Kaminski and used as the basis for a series of silkscreen prints entitled *7 Childlike Uses of Warlike Material* (1971).

A large installation of the same name, composed of a collection of other objects, which were accompanied by inscriptions, was acquired by the Centre Pompidou in 1988 [FIG. 14]. This work was part of the series *A Contribution to the Art of Peace* (1969–1970), an integral component of Filliou's *COMMEMOR* project. Presented at the Neue Galerie in Aachen in 1970, the project reflected the artist's wish to see previously warring countries exchange war memorials in order, among other things, to "remind future generations of the futility and murderous obscenity of nationalism in all its forms."[47]

For the publication, Filliou rewrote the texts accompanying the sculpture. The plates are especially vibrant, combining flat metallic tints with splashes of fluorescent color to produce a composition as playful and joyous as a child's drawing: "a saw could be a submarine; a nail, a missile," and "planks could be mountains, a round rusty piece of metal: the moon." Then, he writes:

I can put the submarine on the mountains.
the missile on the moon. the uniforms around the stars.
the tank in the desert. the guns into the ocean.
the bureaucratic documents in outer space.
I can set the war academy on fire.

It will become
A CONTRIBUTION TO THE ART OF PEACE

47 Centre Pompidou website, accessed on April 28, 2024: https://www.centrepompidou.fr/en/ressources/oeuvre/cnjERq.

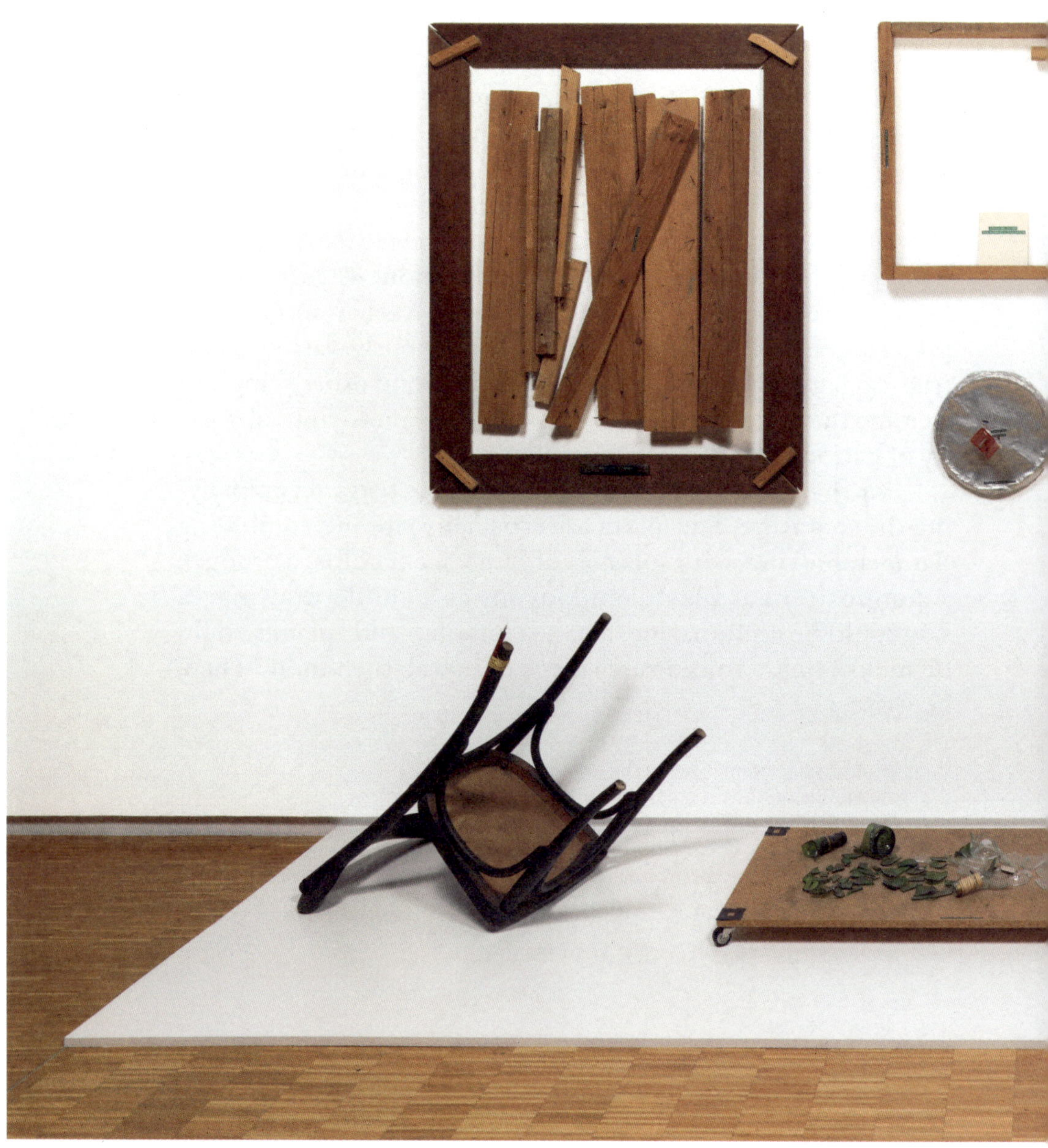

[FIG.14] *7 Childlike Uses of Warlike Material*, 1970
Installation, 182 × 400 × 90 cm
Coll. Centre Georges Pompidou – Musée National d'Art Moderne – Centre de Création Industrielle

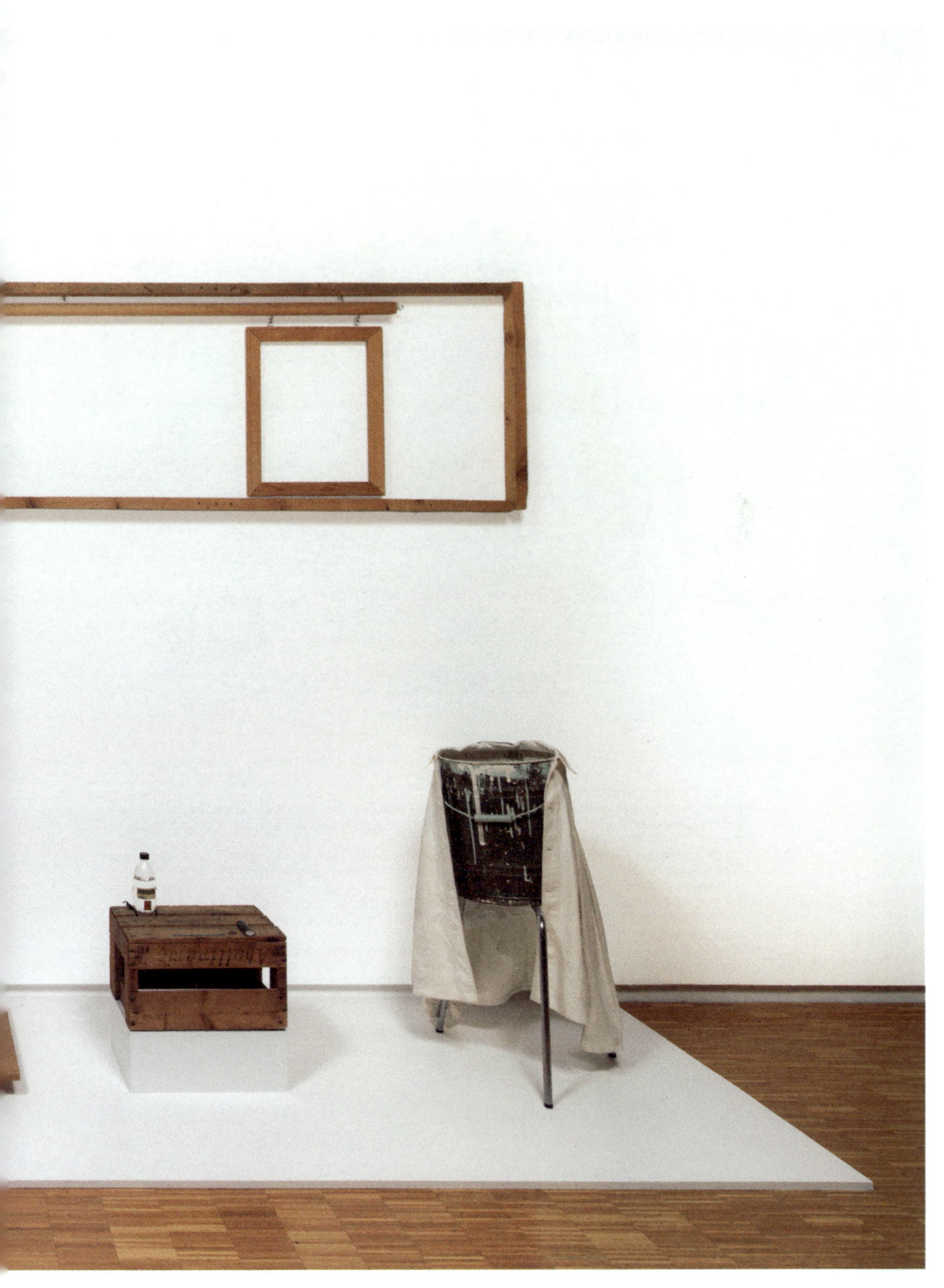

THE FROZEN EXHIBITION

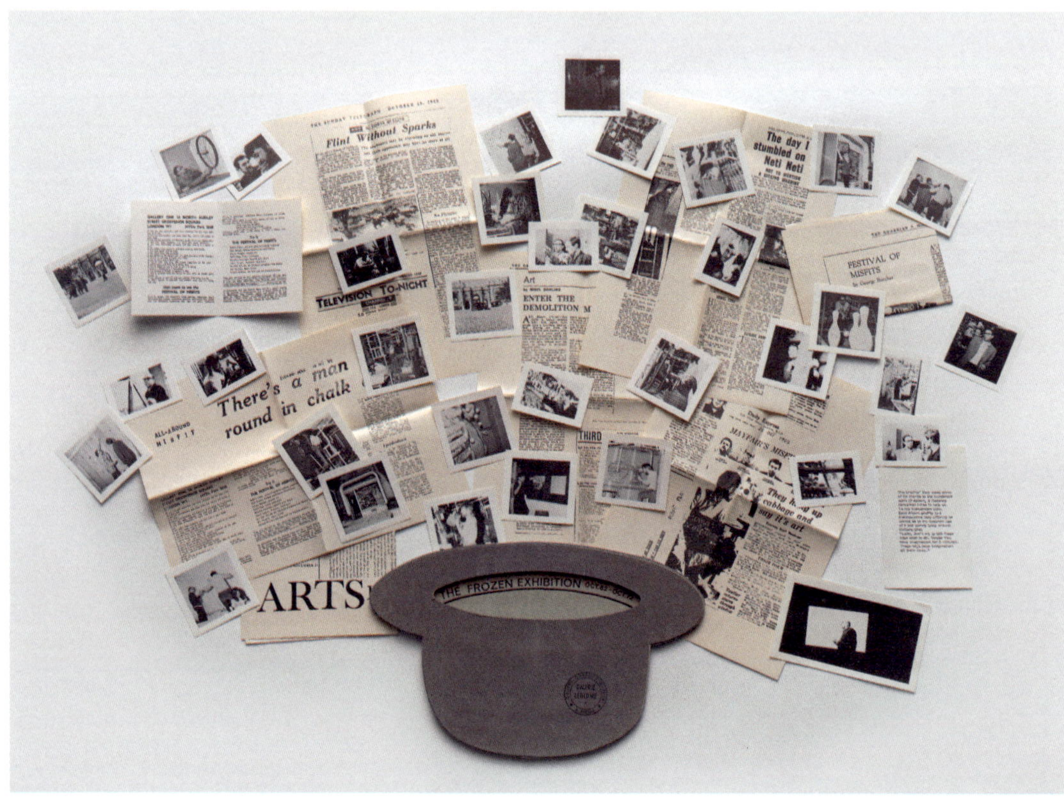

The Frozen Exhibition, Oct. 62–Oct. 72, 1972
Synthetic velvet laminated on cardboard and painted wood, cut in the shape
of a bowler hat, with printed text (front and back) and a *Galerie Légitime* stamp on the
front (20.5 × 31.8 × 0.6 cm), containing:
- 35 black-and-white photographs individually printed on glossy paper in various formats
(8.4 × 14 cm; 7 × 7 cm; 5 × 6.9 cm) with numbered stamps on the back (1 to 35)
- the invitation card for Gallery One, London, printed, single-sided (11.6 × 16.8 cm)
- a note to Albert the carpenter, printed on glossy paper, single-sided
- an invitation to the "Misfits" performance at the ICA, printed on glossy paper,
single-sided
- the press review of *The Misfits' Fair* exhibition: seven standalone pages (21 × 29.7 cm
each), printed on glossy paper, single-sided
VICE-Versand, Remscheid, 170 copies, including 10 copies given to each participant
in *The Misfits' Fair*
signed, lower right, in pencil, below the explanatory text: Rt Filliou
MAMCO collection, bequeathed by Gérald Minkoff and Muriel Olesen

                                                                    Robert Filliou

As part of his *Galerie Légitime* concept, Filliou presented a series of small works by Spoerri, Köpcke, Gustav Metzger, Page, Williams, Ben, and himself under the title *The Frozen Exhibition, Oct. 23, 1962–Oct. 22, 1972*, which ran from October 23 to November 8, 1962. He described it thus:

> THE GALERIE LEGITIME (English version) consisted of a bowler hat, descendant of the several caps and hats in which, since early 1962, I had gone through city streets and inside shops, galleries, and museums, proposing tiny art works for sale (at 5 francs a piece, or in exchange for a drink, if I remember well). The bowler hat containing the artworks was put inside a freezer bag—to underline that the exhibition would not only last for weeks, but for a full 10 years, at the end of which time the bag would be opened and the artworks defrosted. People would then be able to consider in true perspective, not so much the small sample works exhibited by the Galerie Légitime, as their authors, the 7 artists themselves, and the group show that was the occasion for the Frozen Exhibition: The Misfits' Fair.[48]

On October 21, 1972, Filliou held a solo exhibition at Galerie Magers in Bonn. According to the invitation card, the various works on show would include *Defrosting the Frozen Exhibition Oct 23. 1962–Oct 22. 1972*. Filliou announced that, at around midnight, he would defrost the frozen artworks from *The Misfits' Fair*. The title and announcement were, however, misleading because, as Filliou himself explained in this book, the bag placed in a freezer in 1962 had been thrown away by an unknown person in 1964. So instead, that evening, Filliou "defrosted a memory—the memory of the *Galerie Légitime*," presenting the book, published by VICE-Versand,[49] as a way of "recording the event and illustrating the concept" of what was to take place at Galerie Magers. According to its author, the book contained "a cardboard bowler hat, the invitation to *The Misfits' Fair*, 35 photos taken by Bruce Fleming in 1962, the invitation to an ICA performance by the misfits (as the press called us in those days), some snap reactions from the newspapers, an anecdote about Albert the carpenter, and the 'All-Round Misfit' label, handed to each visitor in a small display case as they left the Fair."

Back in 1962, all the artists involved in the project were still unknown and the Fluxus movement was in its infancy. The emerging artistic practices and concepts were not to everybody's liking. The London press was particularly scathing about the show, describing it as an exhibition of "curiosities" by artists "aptly named the Misfits": "[they] hung an old cabbage in a trendy London gallery and called it art"; "also on display were a wet sponge, a bottle opener, an assortment of buttons and handles." Another review noted that the exhibition aimed to "show that art is all around us, if only we would open our eyes to it," but that it had an "aura of charlatanism, of commercialism," while one critic dubbed it the "entry of the wreckers" into the realm of art.

In freezing some of these works, which would otherwise have been destroyed at the end of the exhibition, Filliou wanted to test whether they would be valid after enough time had passed (10 years) for the artists to develop their concepts. An awareness of time, of the long term, was a recurring theme in Filliou's oeuvre. He did not choose the works that were frozen—each participant selected the one they wanted to preserve—but he imagined for them a future that exceeded their intended lifespan. The idea of preserving artworks, using techniques such as mummification, came to Filliou early on in his career: for his very first solo show, held at Galerie Köpcke in Copenhagen, he presented mummified objects and gave a definition of the term.[50] The practice of "encapsulating"[51] the work of other artists can also be seen in his 1968 *Galeries Légitimes*.

---

48   Explanatory typewritten text by Robert Filliou appearing on the back of the publication. The choice of name for the exhibition may have been influenced by John Huston's film *The Misfits*, adapted from Arthur Miller's short story of the same name and released the previous year.

49   The VICE-Versand publishing house was founded in 1968 by Wolfgang Feelisch, a German collector, publisher, and friend and traveling companion of Robert Filliou. He began producing (unlimited) multiples designed by artists close to or belonging to the Fluxus movement. Our translations below.

50   See the earlier discussion of the catalog for Filliou's first exhibition (1961).

51   Andy Warhol's *Time Capsules*, which he began collecting after he was shot by Valérie Solanas in 1968, spring to mind. Speaking about this project, Warhol said: "Everything I do is concerned with death." Unlike Filliou, Warhol did not choose the objects he encapsulated; instead, it was a way for him to preserve anything and everything that passed through his studio.

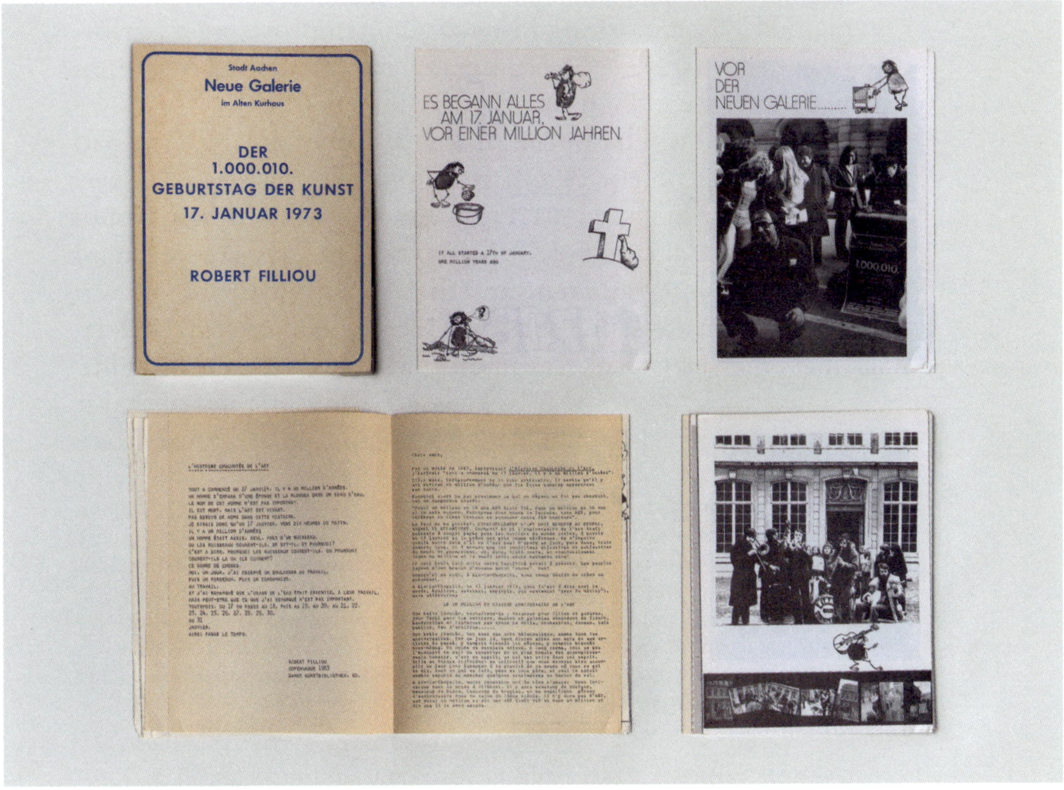

Art's 1,000,010th Birthday, 1973
catalog for the *Art's Birthday* celebrations in Aachen on January 17, 1973
printed sleeve with flaps [55 p.] containing facsimiles of documents, black-and-white illustrations
30.4 × 21.5 cm
Neue Galerie, Aachen
MAMCO collection, bequeathed by Gérald Minkoff and Muriel Olesen

This publication, produced after the event, features texts written by Filliou in German, English and French, including *Whispered Art History*, along with letters, artists' telegrams, press articles and photographs of the festivities held to commemorate Art's 1,000,010th Birthday at Neue Galerie and in the streets of Aachen.

Filliou imagined *Art's Birthday* as a worldwide event that would be celebrated with "international school holidays, paid leave for employees around the world, and spontaneous festivities and merrymaking across the globe… because art must return to the people to whom it belongs." As the artist himself explained: "One morning in 1963, while improvising a performance of *Whispered Art History*, I wrote that it all began on January 17,[52] one million years ago."

The event, a celebration of the fusion of art and life, had a huge impact on the city. It was even mentioned in *Playboy Deutschland*, while the local press announced that there would be "free beer and cake for the birthday party," that there would be music and entertainment, and that "parents with a child born on January 17 should make themselves known to Neue Gallery, as the French artist Robert Filliou will present them with a gift."

Dorothy Iannone, who "witnessed" the event, noted that it was also a celebration of Filliou as a person and as a great artist:

> I was there and I saw it. Robert Filliou, who had refused the Legion of Honor, accepted the Carnival medallion. I will never forget Robert under the immense chandelier, in the center of a huge ring of spectators, with the band and the dancing ladies and Marianne, toasting, laughing, swaying, singing, kissing as cameras reeled and flashbulbs popped and microphones were thrust into the air. The town of Aachen handsomely and generously celebrated—what was it?—I don't think anyone cared. I myself went to celebrate an old friend and an important artist.[53]

Although Filliou's grand plans for *Art's Birthday* (such as having the date declared a public holiday in every country around the world) did not come to fruition, the event has become a very real success: it has since spread to Canada, the United Kingdom, Portugal, France, Switzerland, and beyond, with various festivities taking place each year to celebrate the artist and art itself.

52   Contrary to Filliou's own assertion, the choice of date was not arbitrary: January 17 was his birthday. Our translation, here and below.

53   "Letter from Dorothy Iannone" in *Robert Filliou: The Secret of Permanent Creation*, exhibition catalog, M HKA, 2017, p. 22.

INFORMATION BOX

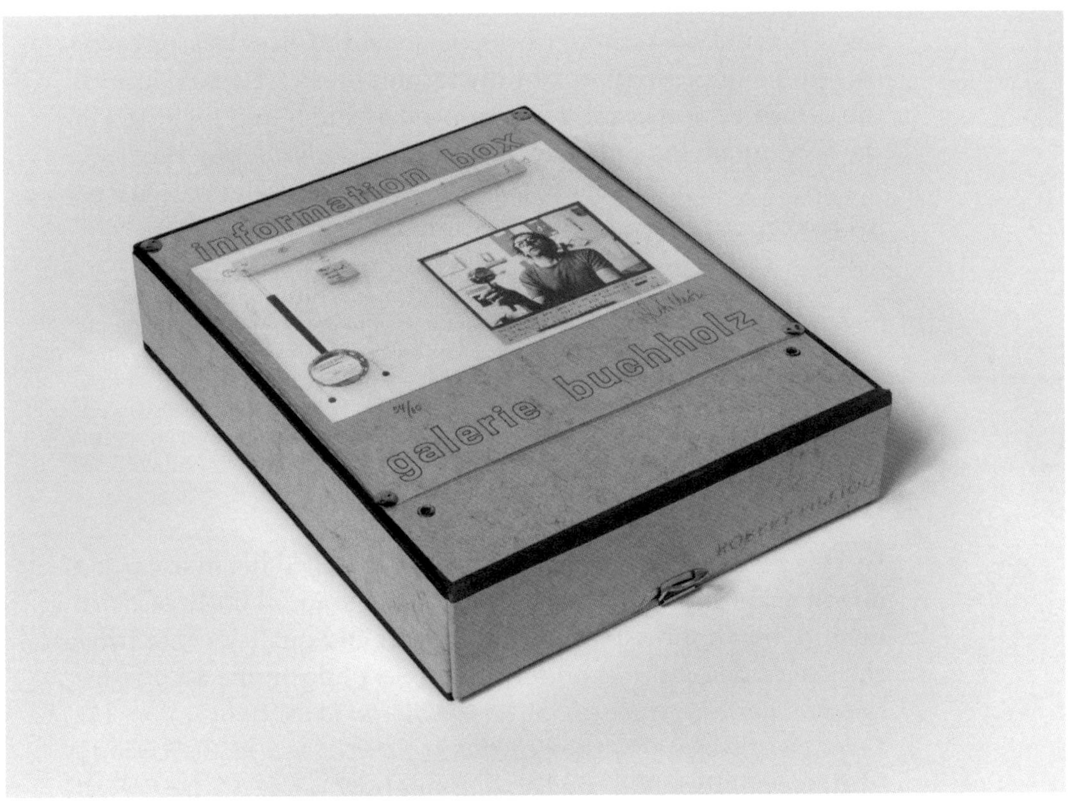

Information Box, 1973
reinforced cardboard storage box, lined at the corners and displaying, in a pinned plastic
sleeve, a black-and-white photograph of the work *That Spiritual Need*. It contains seven
publications (originals, stamped "Information Box"):
George Brecht and Robert Filliou, *Games at the Cedilla, or the Cedilla Takes Off*, Something
Else Press, New York, 1967
Robert Filliou & Cie, *Poème collectif*, Daily-Bul, La Louvière, 1968
Robert Filliou *Lehren und Lernen als Aufführungskünste/Teaching and Learning as
Performing Arts*, Verlag Gebr. König, Cologne, 1970
Robert Filliou Commemor Nr. 4, Neue Galerie, Aachen, July-Dec., 1970
Robert Filliou, Galerie René Block, Berlin, 1971
Robert Filliou, *Ein Sublimat aus 1000 Gedichte japanisch*, Galerie der Spiegel, Cologne, 1971
Filliou, catalog, Galerie Buchholz, Munich, 1973
24 slides in a Plexiglas case (numbered 001 to 024) and a set of texts and photocopies of
invitation cards contained in a plastic sleeve with a metal slide clip
Galerie Buchholz, Munich, 60 copies
32.8 × 25.5 × 7.2 cm
MAMCO collection

Information Box was produced by Galerie Buchholz in Munich to coincide with its Filliou exhibition. The show featured 38 works produced between 1968 and 1973, categorized as follows in the catalog: "isolated works; joint works; personalized messages; research on filmmaking; portraits not made; and boxes." Twenty-four of the exhibited works were reproduced as slides and included in the accompanying publication, also titled *Information Box*.

In a text penned for the exhibition catalog, Filliou discussed his concept of "Permanent Creation":

> About 10 years ago, I developed the "concept of permanent creation" for my own needs. It was—at least for me—a necessity to be creative at all times; not to be influenced by anything, not even by my previous ideas, to keep my mind always open and, in my art, to be as spontaneous as I wanted to be…. I have produced a series of works that should not be viewed solely for their visual content, which is very important…What I am really trying to do, what is important to me, is to create spontaneously, to communicate my emotions—or whatever else it may be—as spontaneously as possible.[54]

By this point, Filliou was 47 and had produced his first work a dozen years earlier. He already had a substantial body of work behind him, impressive in both number and quality, cementing the key principles that underpinned his philosophy: *L'Autrisme* (1962), *Galerie Légitime* (1962), *La Cédille qui sourit* (1965–1968), *The Eternal Network* (1968), the *Principle of Equivalence* (1968), *Territory of the Genial Republic*, the *Poïpoïdrome* (1970) and COMMEMOR (1970). His seminal work, *Teaching and Learning as Performing Arts*, was published by König's publishing house, in 1970. The first *Art's Birthday* celebrations had recently taken place in Aachen, and *Recherche sur l'origine/Research on the Origin* was a work in progress. Filliou lived in Germany, where he enjoyed the support of galleries such as Schmela, René Block, and Buchholz. German publishers were loyal to him, and many of his collectors were also German. The previous year, he had participated in *documenta 5* in Kassel, and held a number of exhibitions. He was at a point in his life where he felt the need to bring together the sum total of his research, experience and philosophy in one place.

With his recently published work *Research in Dynamics and Comparative Statics* (1972–1973), he had started the process of consolidating his poetry (1958–1965) by placing facsimiles of his manuscripts and typescripts, along with an audio recording, in a wooden suitcase. This approach bears many similarities with Marcel Duchamp's boxes,[55] although Filliou's suitcase was more unassuming in appearance and more in line with his ongoing predilection for a nomadic lifestyle.

Three of the publications that Filliou included in his *Information Box* marked important milestones in his life.

La Cédille qui sourit was a "non-shop-studio" in Villefranche-sur-Mer run by Filliou and Brecht between 1965 and 1968. *Games at the Cedilla, or the Cedilla Takes Off* details the activities of the two artists and their partners, Marianne Staffeldt and Donna Brewer, during this period.

> Not registered as a company and only open by demand, [*La Cédille qui sourit*] was the first Centre of Permanent Creation for new games—so we put a little arrow to *Games"—inventing and dis-inventing objects, fabricating suspense poems and magazines intended for mail order.[56]

The book is a first-hand narrative interwoven with *One-Minute Scenarios*, games, letters, reflections on marriage and sexuality, and articles – including one in which Filliou and Brecht mention their shared ambition to make Villefranche-sur-Mer an art destination: "a Villefranche of the Arts."

In the same year the book was published, Jacqueline Ranson's Galerie J in Paris held an exhibition organized by *La Cédille qui sourit*. The show was billed as offering "something unexpected": works by around 60 artists, some produced in Villefranche-sur-Mer, and some that Filliou would later use for his *Galeries Légitimes*. The exhibited artists came from a variety of backgrounds—Abstractionists, Situationists, and members of the Fluxus movement—and included such unexpected names as Mosset, Agnès Varda, and Maurice Henry.

Lehren und Lernen als Aufführungskünste/Teaching and Learning as Performing Arts [FIG. 16]
Verlag Gebr. König, Cologne, 1970

Filliou wrote this bilingual (German and English) "multi-book" between 1967 and 1970. It gives an overview of the main projects he had completed at the time.

Filliou believed that intuition, innocence, imagination and the creative use of leisure held the key to closing the gap between artist and audience and bringing the two together in a process of

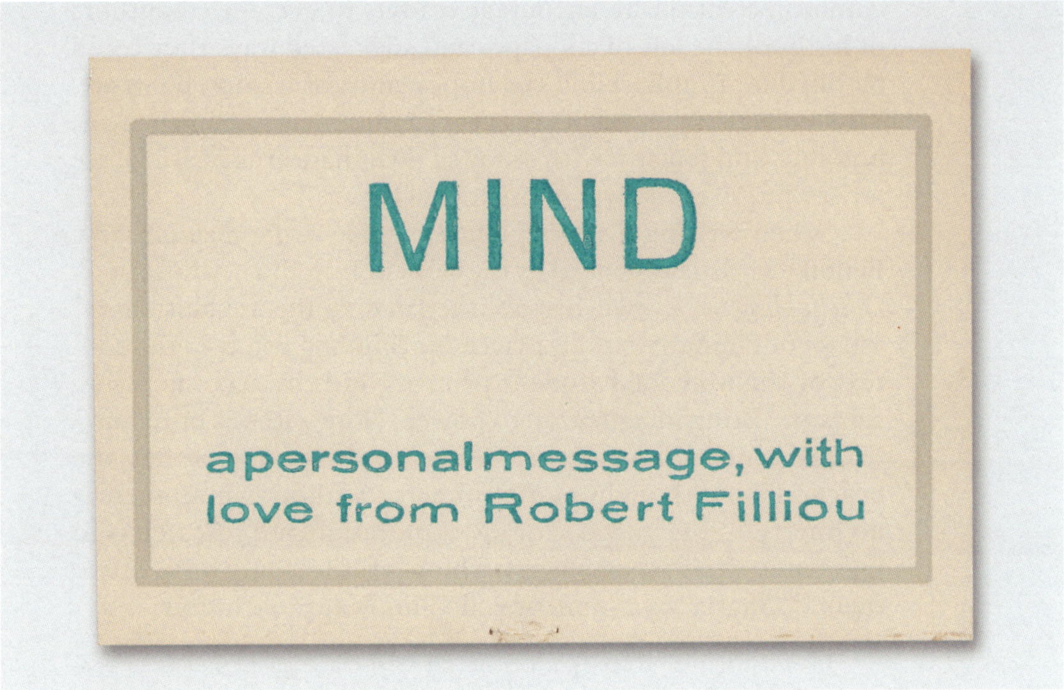

[FIG. 15] *Mind*, 1971
Offset print, 10.9 × 15.9 cm, ed. Angela Flowers Gallery, London
Coll. MAMCO, legs Gérald et Muriel Minkoff-Olesen

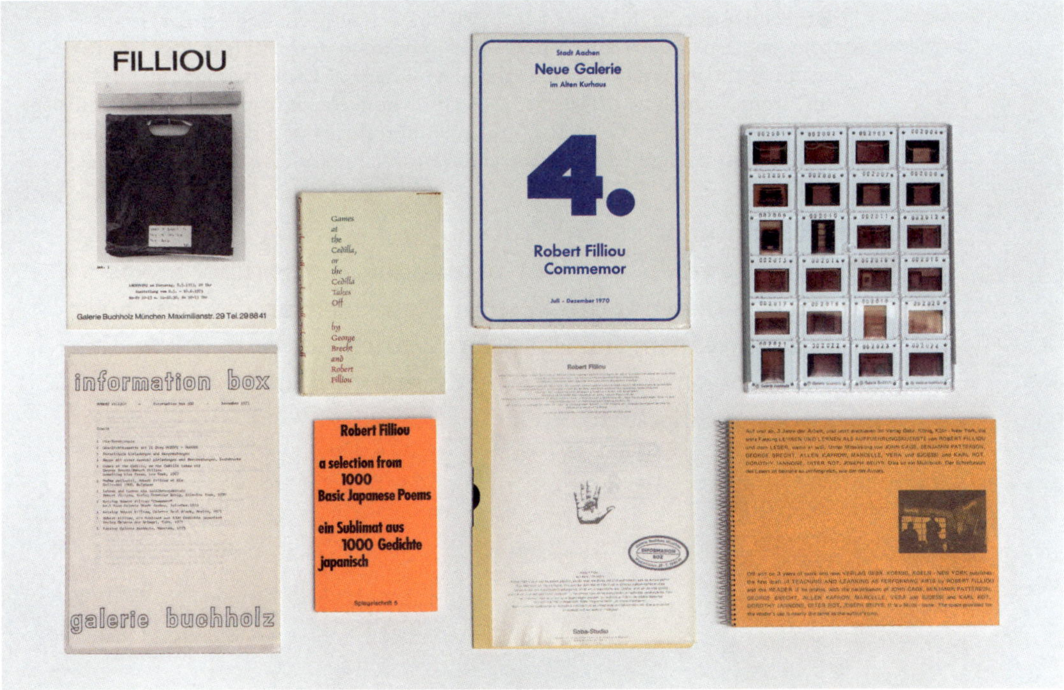

[FIG. 16] Publications from *Information Box*

common creation. To encourage readers to become co-authors of his book, he left blank pages and suggested ways they could be filled in. Emphasizing the importance of leisure, he wrote: "The only group of adults that try to obtain as much leisure as possible, and to use it with as much imagination as possible, are artists. [...] Art is a form of organized leisure."[57]

When writing *Teaching and Learning as Performing Arts*, Filliou was also influenced by the work of Ivan Illich, whose book *Deschooling Society* will be published in 1971. The "revolutionary" aspect of Filliou's writings placed his thinking firmly in the context of the May 1968 student protests and the accompanying slogans: "Bring imagination to power," "Life without boredom," "Enjoyment without limits," "Beneath the paving stones, the beach." Filliou thought of the workers, "without whom there is no poetry": "The purpose of my exploration and research is to find out in what aspect poetry, which is futile, could be useful to them."[58] Sharla Sava summarized Filliou's approach thus:

> In certain European circles, artists mounted resistance against the nascent consumer culture in different ways: Filliou's contact with the New Realists, with Jean-Clarence Lambert's 'Domaine Poétique' in Paris, and with the Fluxus actions and performances that took place in Europe and the United States starting in 1962, place him firmly among the enclaves of bohemian cultural opposition that were active during this period. Inspired by Duchamp and Cage, these groups—some more coherent than others—had a common desire to bring art into the realm of the everyday. Filliou is the playful hero of Lambert's 1971 manifesto on "arters," which he defines as "those for whom the pure meaning of artistic activity has undergone such a fundamental transformation that they can no longer be considered artists in any conventional sense."[59]

In 1979, Filliou produced *Teaching and Learning as Performing Arts Part II*, a video follow-up to his book. At the time, he was an artist-in-residence at the Western Front art center in Vancouver under a grant from the Canadian Conference of the Arts. This environment served as a new medium for Filliou's actions, conversations and performances:

I intend to see if it is possible to put into practice what I proposed a decade or more ago as an artistic technique […] or as a way of living art, or of treating life as art, what I called "teaching and learning as performing arts." In this sense, everything is performance.[60]

COMMEMOR (Joint Commission for the Exchange of War Memorials)

"Established in July 1970 at Neue Galerie in Aachen with the aim of solemnly offering the peoples of Europe the opportunity to exchange their respective war memorials. As for countries considering waging war today, instead of fighting each other, they could exchange their memorials to those who lost their lives in previous conflicts." Filliou was, of course, a committed pacifist. He and Josef Beuys met the Dalai Lama in 1982 for a "Peace Biennial" project, and he worked with students in Hamburg on the *Peace* project. In 1985, Filliou and Marianne embarked on a three-year retreat at the Centre d'Etudes de Chanteloube, a center for Tibetan studies in the Dordogne region of France. There, he rubbed shoulders with British scientist Bernard Benson who, in the 1950s, had made a career out of designing weapons for the United States. After moving to Saint-Léon-sur Vézère, Benson discovered Buddhism and became a pacifist. In 1980, he published *The Peace Book*, a story for children and adults.

54   *Filliou*, Galerie Buchholz, Munich, exhibition catalog, May 8–June 16, 1973, n.p. Our translation.

55   Sylvie Jouval draws a parallel between *Research in Dynamics and Comparative Statics* and Duchamp's *The Green Box*, in *op. cit.*, p. 64.

56   *Robert Filliou: The Secret of Permanent Creation*, M HKA, *op. cit*, p. 31.

57   Robert Filliou, *Teaching and Learning as Performing Arts*, Verlag Gebr. König, Cologne/New York, 1970, pp. 21 and 23.

58   *Porta Filliou*, a video primer summarizing Filliou's artistic practice and ideas, 1977. Our translation.

59   Sharla Sava, "Les bandes Filliou – de l'Economie Politique à l'Economie poétique," in *Robert Filliou: From Political to Poetical Economy*, Morris and Helen Belkin Art Gallery, Vancouver, 1996, p. 25. Our translation.

60   https://mediation.centrepompidou.fr/education/ressources/ENS-Filliou/#performing. Our translation.

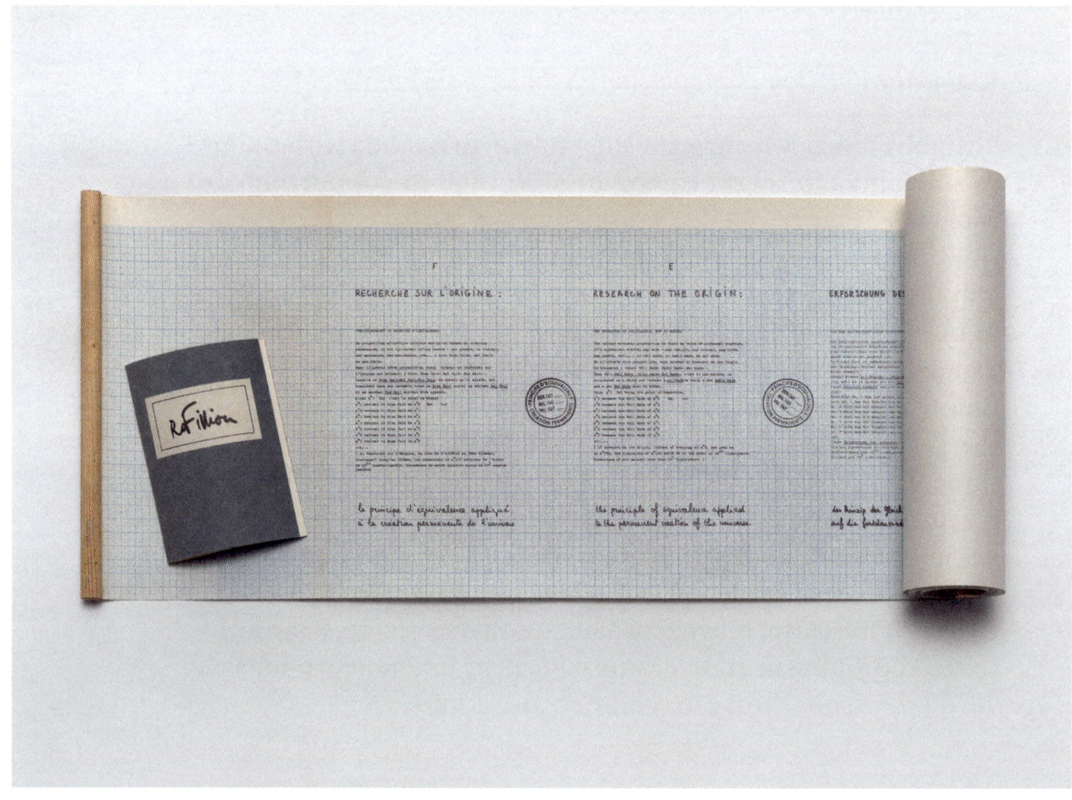

Research on the Origin, 1974
offset-printed publication on a millimeter-graph-paper scroll held in place by two circular wooden rods, accompanied by a booklet [40 p.], all contained in a cardboard box; 30 x 1018 cm (when unrolled)
Städtischen Kunsthalle, Düsseldorf, 400 copies
MAMCO collection, acquired through the MAMCO Friends Association

Research on the Origin started out life as a piece of fabric measuring 2.75 meters tall and 89 meters long on which Filliou drew and wrote in oil pastel during his time as an artist-in-residence with the German Academic Exchange Service (DAAD) in Berlin. This monumental work from 1974 has been described as "a flexible canvas[61] on which Filliou develops his idea of permanent creation and the associated principle of equivalence—well made/badly made/not made—which he applies to creation in general and to the human race in particular: creation of the world and creation of man."[62]

In the same year, the Kunsthalle Düsseldorf published a miniaturized version of the work, reduced to 1:10 scale, in a run of 450 copies (including 50 for the artist). Its form—eight sheets of millimeter graph paper laid end-to-end to form a scroll, held at each end by a circular wooden rod—was reminiscent of ancient scrolls from different parts of the world.

In a piece about *Research on the Origin*,[63] Jean-Christophe Ammann recalls Filliou's account of his discussion with mathematician Warren Hirsch—a conversation that led the artist to draw a possible comparison between his body of work and the sciences:

> In February 1967, I went to dinner at [the home of] my friend the mathematician Warren Hirsh, who teaches and does research work at New York University. John Cage drove Marianne and me to his place. It is during this ride that John told me we should, in social matters, achieve the equivalent of getting rid of harmony and counterpoint in music. [...] That evening I asked Warren what he was presently working on. He answered that it had to do with some complex mathematical problems exploring the possibility of "building perfect wholes out of imperfect parts." It concerned circuits, of course. As I understood what he said, if [in] a circuit composed of many components, one of them breaks down, the whole circuit stops. But if each component itself reproduces the whole circuit, with all its components, and each of these in turn reproduce the whole circuit, and so on and so on, we may arrive at a total circuit that will never break down, no matter if any or some of its components do. It made me think of the human brain, of memory, for instance. You may try to remember somebody's name by calling to mind his face. If it does not work, recall of making his acquaintance may bring up his name. Or odd association of ideas, having to do with sounds, smells, objects, etc.... In most cases, some components of the brain fail, and yet the answer will come out: the brain does his work. [...] I told Warren: "That's exactly what I try to discover in the fields of art, education and social matters." Yes it is.

Research on the Origin also draws on Filliou's Principle of Equivalence—the notion, conceived in 1968, that "well made," "badly made" and "not made" were all equivalent.

> I am interested in permanent creation. I can manipulate this concept and use it everywhere in my work. Here's a stamp I once had bearing the words: Permanent Creation – Principle of Equivalence: Well Made. Badly Made. Not Made. This means that, in terms of permanent creation, it matters not whether a work is

well made, badly made or not made. All three are equivalent. I became interested in permanent creation, and I used that term more than the word "art," because it is creativity that interests me… *The Principle of Equivalence* is a kind of conceptual tool that I have used in many of my works. The first of these was a red sock in a yellow box whose proportions and colors were just right—I called this work "well made." Then I made it again, but this time the proportions and color were wrong—"badly made"—so I made it a third time… I found these works to be well made given the effort they had required. I then redid all three of them as badly made, and a third time as not made… I had to stop at the fifth item in the series because it was already 40 feet long. I calculated that a series of 100 would extend to 10 light years (to the power of 21). And every time I have shown this work, I have said that it uses the permanent creation of the universe.[64]

For Jean-Hubert Martin, the Principle of Equivalence is akin to Conceptual art:

Research on the Origin and the Principle of Equivalence are based on similar premises. The Principle of Equivalence hinges on the triptych of "well made," "badly made" and "not made." Intellectually speaking, it is curiously reminiscent of Stakhanovite dialectics. From a formal perspective, it sets in motion a process of exponential growth. It is interesting to note both a concern with escaping the binary system that underpins most Western thinking, and a similarity with Lawrence Weiner's statement: "the work need not be built; the work may be fabricated; an artist may construct the work."[65]

In 1975, Filliou's Berlin-based friends Robert Rehfeldt and his partner Ruth Wolf-Rehfeldt held an exhibition in honor of the artist at the EP Gallery in East Berlin. Alongside works by Karlheinz Schäfer, Hans Brosch, Hartmut Bonk, A. R. Penck, and Robert Rehfeldt, the show featured Filliou's *Research on the Origin*, "a scroll that, when unrolled, measured over 9 meters in length. The entire scroll could be seen in the gallery, held in place by clothes pins suspended from wires. Filliou was present at the opening, sporting a bright yellow sweater."[66] Gallery owner Jürgen Schweinebraden wrote:

Robert's artistic ideas were barely perceptible to us, and we understood very little of what he was telling us. His idea of art seemed to us like the other side of the moon, very far away, very foreign. Such a vision, so far removed from the aesthetic categories of our time, was interesting in itself and piqued our curiosity. Compared to the situation with traditional Western art circles and the social and political upheavals that rocked their foundations, we felt like thirsty sponges permanently relegated to the edge of the basin.[67]

61   Filliou retrieved entire rolls of unbleached fabric from the Berlin State Opera, where they had been used on set. He would later use these pieces of fabric as the medium for many of his works.

62   Description of the work on the Musée d'art contemporain de Lyon website: https://www.navigart.fr/mac-lyon/artwork/robert-filliou-recherche-sur-l-origine-8000000 0000251. Our translation.

63   Jean-Christophe Ammann, in *Spiralen und Progressionen*, exhibition catalog, which reproduces the text originally published in *Lehren und Lernen als Aufführungskünste/Teaching and Learning as Performing Arts*.

64   https://www.navigart.fr/mac-lyon/artwork/robert-filliou-recherche-sur-l-origine-8000000000251. Our translation.

65   Jean-Hubert Martin, "*Robert Filliou: sans artifice,*" in *Robert Filliou*, Editions Lebeer Hossmann, Brussels, 1990, p. 54. Our translation.

66   Frédéric Vincent, *Robert Filliou. La fragilité des choses*, Immanences éditions, Paris, 2023, n.p. Our translation.

67   Jürgen Schweinebraden Freiherr von Wichmann-Eichborn, in *Robert Filliou*, Editions Lebeer Hossmann, Brussels, 1990, pp. 207–208. Our translation.

BOUT DU MONDE, JARDIN D'EDEN

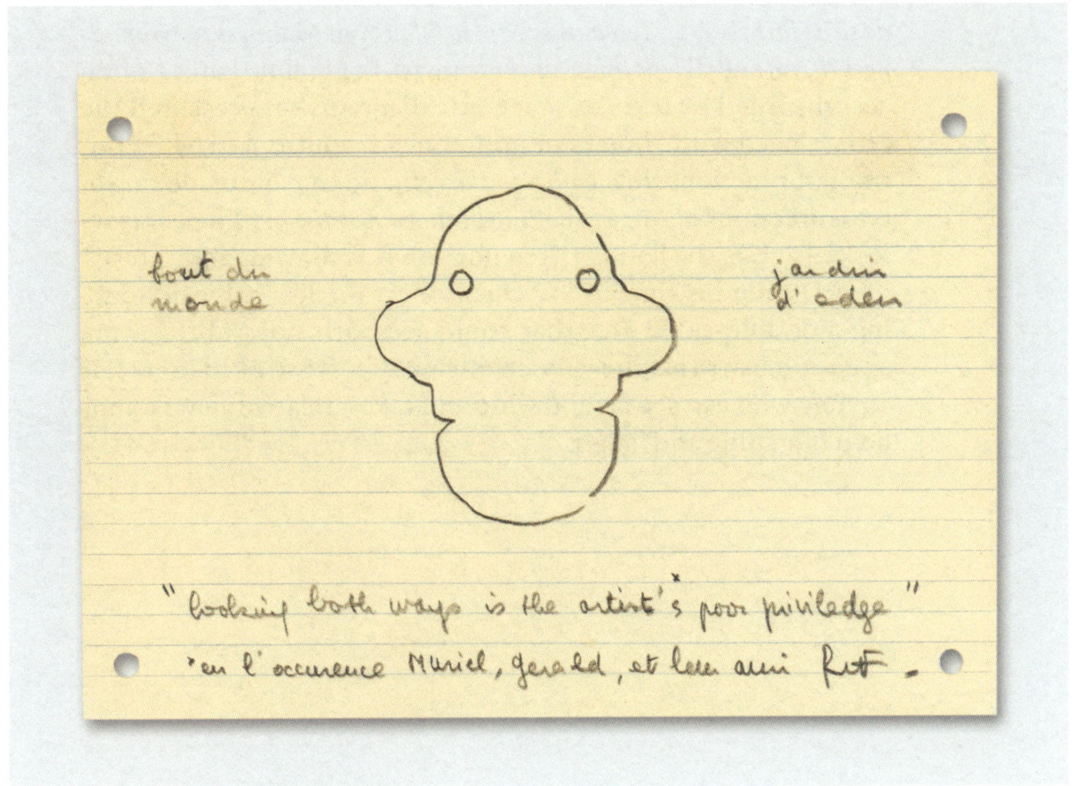

Bout du monde, Jardin d'Eden, c. 1974
graphite on card stock; 14.8 × 21 cm
MAMCO collection, bequeathed by Gérald Minkoff and Muriel Olesen

Filliou used simple, inexpensive materials. Many of the invitation cards and drawings he incorporated into his works were executed on small pieces of lined or squared card that were readily available in stores—the same cards that some galleries used to catalog and classify works in the pre-digital age.

In this hastily sketched drawing for his friends Muriel Olesen and Gérald Minkoff, Filliou depicted the two faces of Janus in the center of the card. The Roman god would become a recurring figure in the artist's work: it appeared in chalk on a brick for *La Nostalgie du souvenir* (1980–1984), and was pasted or drawn onto a strip of fabric for *Faim: fin de la faim – Fin: faim de la fin – Suivi de sans faim* (1982), *Telepathic Music N°: From Madness to Nomadness* (1979) and *Telepathic Sculpture* (1975). For Filliou, Janus—often accompanied by texts or schematic diagrams—represented the artist: faced with choices or non-choices, confronted with contradictory actions *(Remember to Forget)*, and capable of looking in two directions at once *(Looking both ways is the artist's poor priviledge* [sic], as the handwritten note on this drawing indicates).[68]

"During his time in Flayosc, Robert made a habit of drawing a double-sided face that could see both sides of the same situation. Isn't this the very definition of a sense of humor? For anyone who can see far and wide and take a relative view cannot help but smile and laugh."[69]

68   "I believe very deeply—my deepest intuition—is that I am a harmonizer. Naturally, and generally, I've represented this with the phrase 'looking both ways is the poet's poor privilege.'" Excerpt from a 1984 interview with Georg Jappe, quoted in *Robert Filliou*, Editions Lebeer Hossmann, *op. cit.*, p. 156. Our translation.

69   Pierre Tilman, *op. cit*, p. 231.

A MOST CURIOUS INVENTION OF THE GAGA YOGI

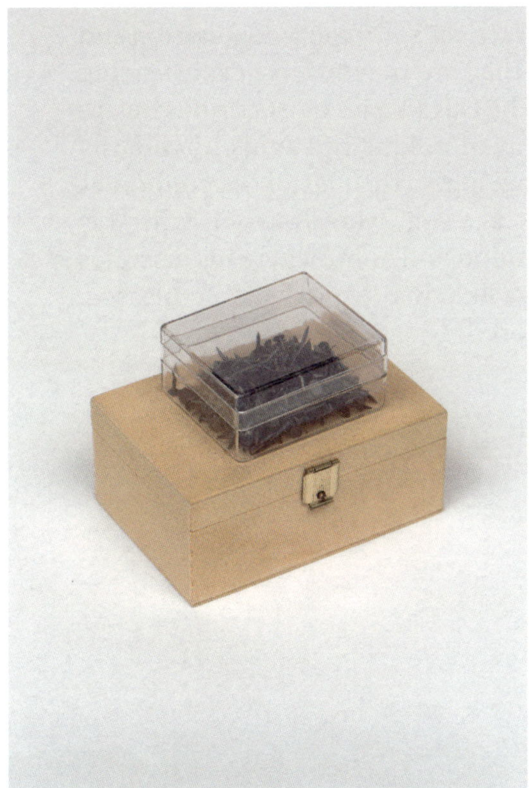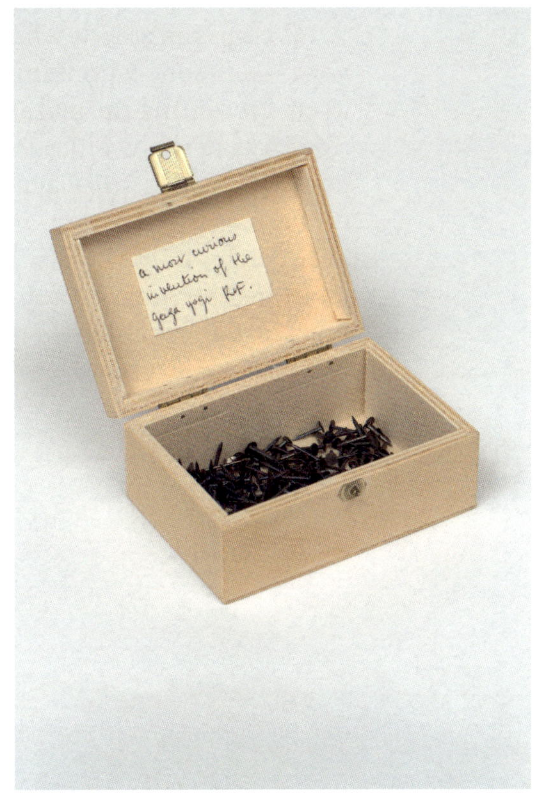

A Most Curious Invention of the Gaga Yogi, 1976
wood, nails, plastic, print on paper; 7.4 × 10.7 × 8 cm
Armin Hundertmark, Cologne, 100 copies
MAMCO collection, bequeathed by Gérald Minkoff and Muriel Olesen

The Gaga Yogi was Filliou's alter ego[70]—a figure who liked to hang out with the clueless, preferred armchair philosophy to ready-made ideas, was interested in the science of "stupidology," and could trace his artistic lineage back to the 19th-century Incoherents. For Filliou, idiocy was a third way, an alternative to facing up to his problems. Humor gave him a spring in his step, offering a positive release of energy. He saw farce, gags and pranks as a way of responding to oppression—a much-needed outlet for a man who forever oscillated between the funny and the pathetic. Marianne Filliou once said of Filliou that "the world pains him": for him, humor was a way of coping with this sickness.[71]

A yogi is an ascetic who practices spirituality, meditation and yoga—someone who knows they are the universe experiencing itself. Presenting the nail as "the Gaga Yogi's most curious invention" was perhaps Filliou's way of poking fun at his legendarily poor DIY skills. "The Gaga Yogi is also the master of ceremonies for Permanent Creation. The Gaga Yogi, who always loses his way between his home in East London and Soho, where his disciples await his teaching, says things like this: 'Now that I am blessed, I feel just as miserable as before.'"[72]

70   "'Gaga Yogi'... It's a way of describing what George and I spoke about in *Teaching and Learning as Performing Arts*," said Filliou. "Since then, I think I am the only one to use it and characterise myself as Gaga Yogi." *Robert Filliou: The Secret of Permanent Creation*, op. cit., p. 182.

71   It is said that when the Dalai Lama was forced to flee Lhasa across snow-covered mountains in 1959, he spent the journey teasing his companions about the way they rode and joking about their brightly colored outfits, for he knew that only laughter would save his fellow travelers from despair, and he had nothing else to offer them. Cited by Pierre Tilman, *op. cit.*, p. 259.

72   *The Eternal Network Presents: Robert Filliou*, exhibition catalog, *op. cit.*, p. 79. Our translation.

POUSSIÈRE DE POUSSIÈRE DE L'EFFET…

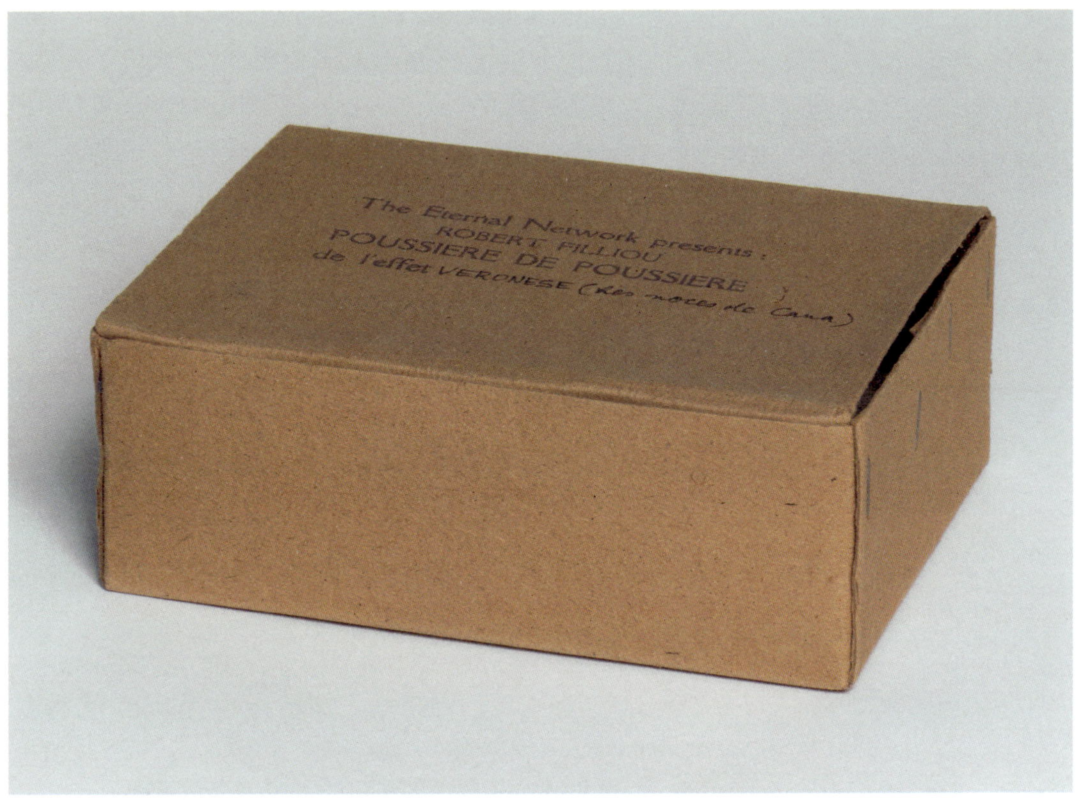

Poussière de poussière de l'effet…, 1977
cardboard box, cloth and Polaroid (taken by Daniel Spoerri)
6 × 16.5 × 12 cm (box closed) / 14.5 × 16.5 × 23 cm (box open)
6.3 × 21 × 17 cm (box closed) / 17 × 21 × 32.5 cm (box open)

Each work in this series, produced in May 1977, follows the same model: Filliou placed a used dust cloth in a cardboard box.[73] He had used the cloths in question to clean around 100 classical, modern and contemporary paintings and sculptures at two leading Parisian museums—an act that would otherwise have been forbidden had he not received permission from Jean-Hubert Martin (then head of collections at the Musée National d'Art Moderne) and Jean-Pierre Cuzin (then chief curator of paintings at the Louvre).[74] Inside each

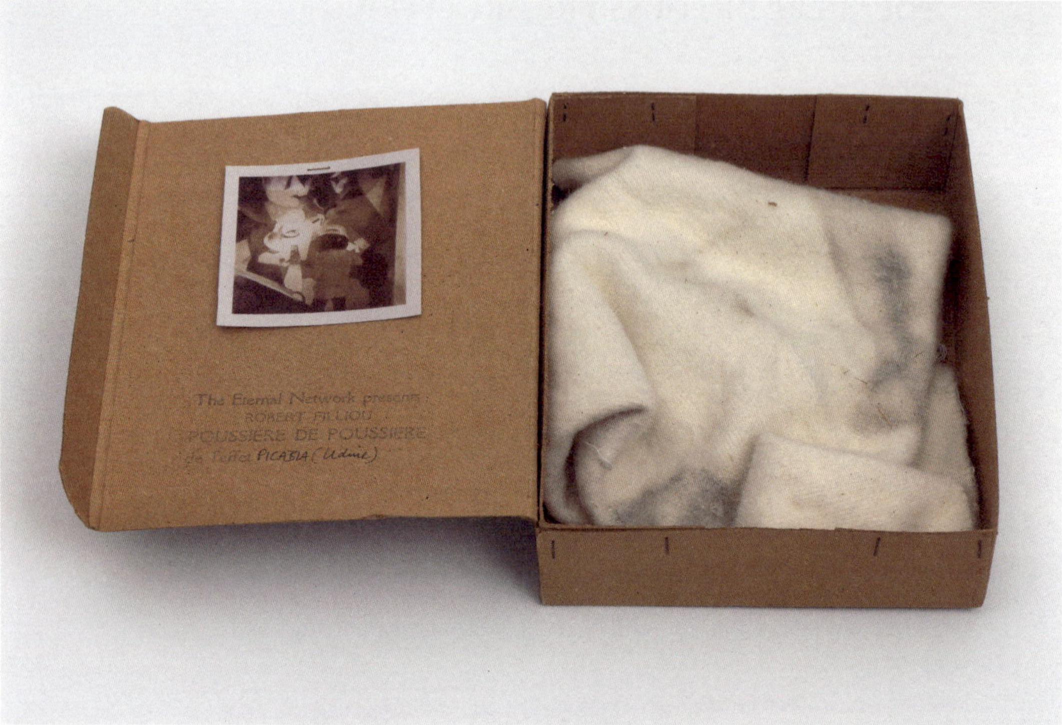

The Eternal Network presents
ROBERT FILLIOU
POUSSIÈRE DE POUSSIÈRE
de l'effet PICABIA (Udnie)

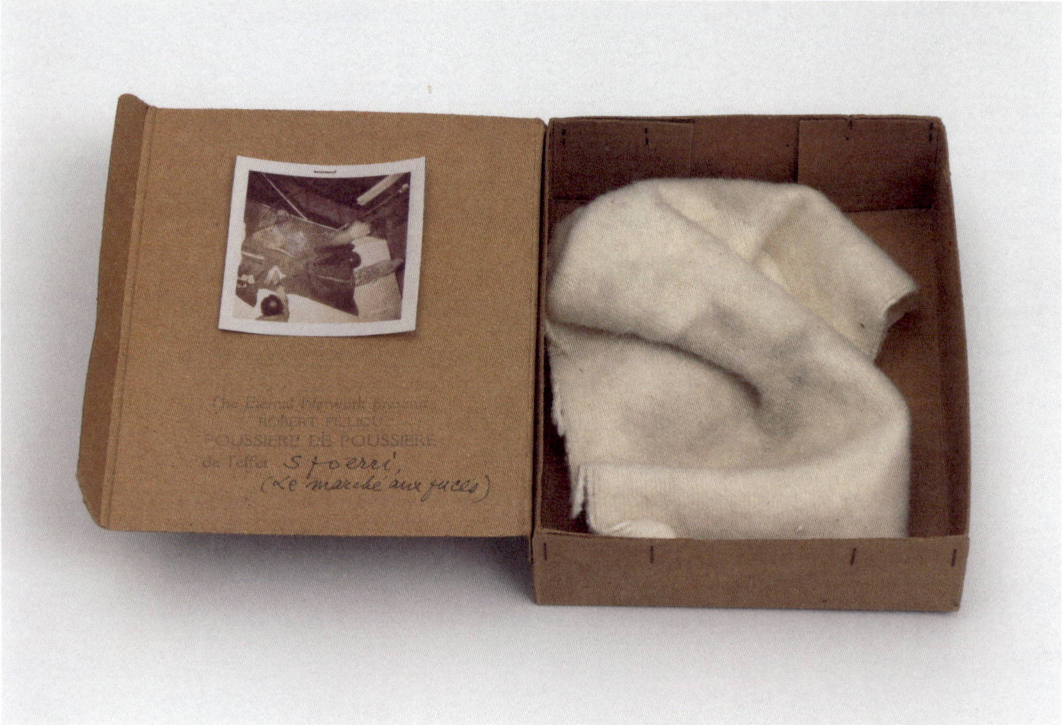

The Eternal Network presents
ROBERT FILLIOU
POUSSIÈRE DE POUSSIÈRE
de l'effet Spoerri
(Le marché aux puces)

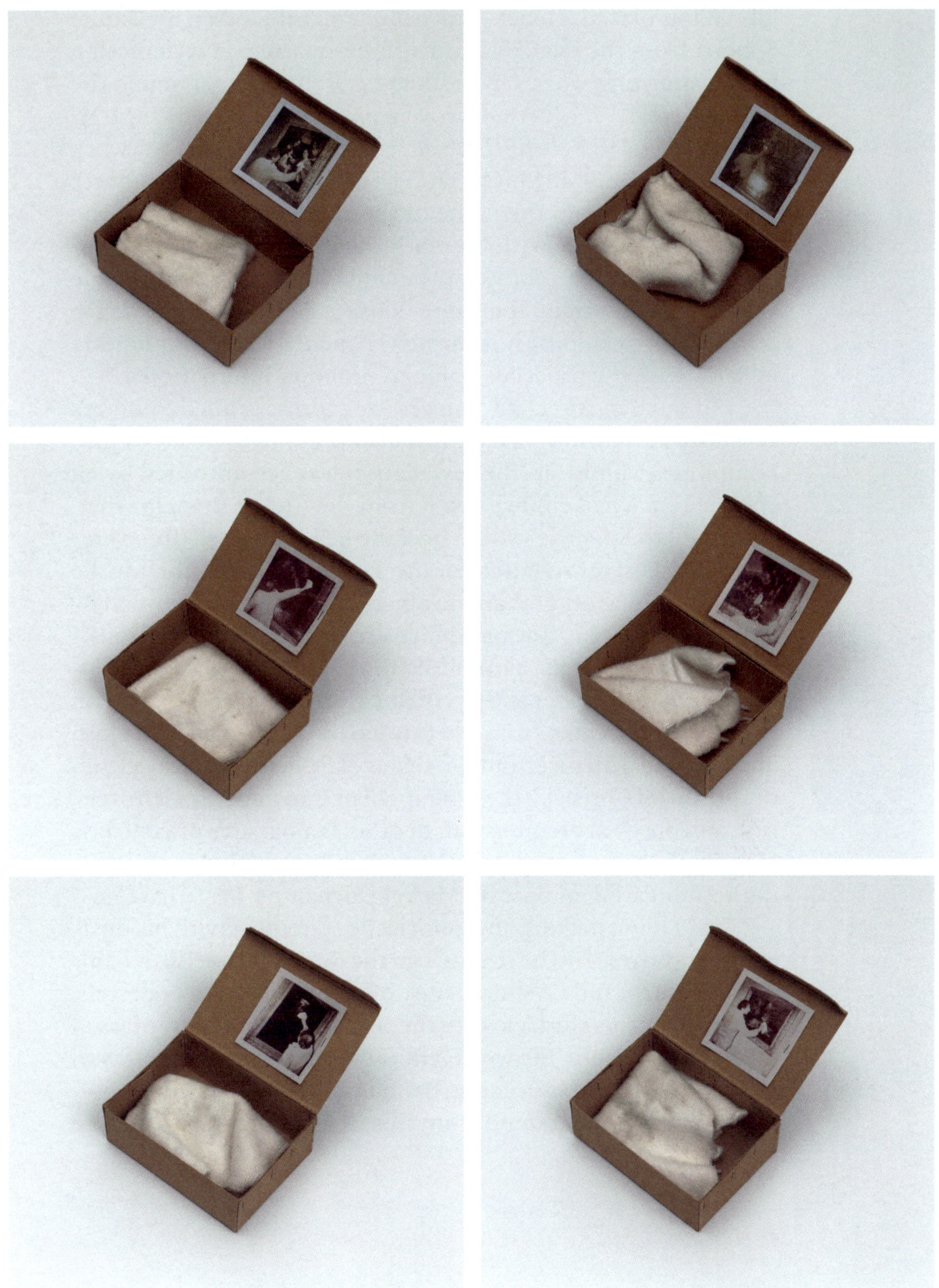

lid, Filliou placed a black-and-white Polaroid, taken by Daniel Spoerri from the back or from a three-quarter view, depicting him dusting off a work. On the outside of the lid, he stamped the following text: "*The Eternal Network présente: ROBERT FILLIOU POUSSIERE DE POUSSIERE de l'effet…*" (The Eternal Network presents: ROBERT FILLIOU DUST TO DUST from the…effect). Filliou then wrote in the name of the artist and the title of the work he had cleaned with the cloth. Each item in the series, produced in around 100 copies, was unique. The boxes went on sale at Spoerri's "Boutique aberrante" kiosk at *Le Crocrodrome de Zig et Puce*, a 1977 exhibition at the newly opened Centre Pompidou in Paris, with the proceeds going to Amnesty International.[75]

Filliou's *Poussières de poussière de l'effet…* echoed Spoerri's *Le Musée sentimental,* which was also presented at the Centre Pompidou exhibition. The installation was accompanied by an ephemeron: a nail clipper taken from the Atelier Brancusi that, according to Spoerri, "would become […] the vehicle for everything Brancusi represented for me. Fetishism, no doubt, for the fetish is nothing other than the object that activates the mind by its mere presence."[76] The pamphlet also included a description of another object Spoerri had collected: a circular reliquary, measuring 22.5 cm in diameter and 5.5 cm thick, which was said to contain "a rosary of olive pits from the Garden of Gethsemane," "a cloth impregnated with rust from the chains of St. Peter" and "dust from the prison [of Christ?]." These scraps of next to nothing—leftovers, rust, and dust—are reminiscent of other famous artworks such as Man Ray's 1920 photograph *Dust Breeding,* which documented the accumulation of dust on Marcel Duchamp's *The Large Glass.*

Was Filliou making an iconoclastic statement with his dust-cloths-in-boxes? Did he really clean the works, at the risk of damaging them, or did he simply dust off the frames and pedestals, only bringing his cloth close to the surface when Spoerri pressed the shutter button? The word "effect" in the series' title refers to an event produced by a cause, or an impression made on someone. Are we to understand from this that artworks have a finite lifespan—for their destiny is to crumble into dust—and that their fetishization is nothing more than an illusion? Or did Filliou find amusement in the fact that, by gathering dust from "master-pieces," he was raising money for a humanitarian cause—which, for him, was precisely the role of art? After all, as he said himself, "I don't care if art doesn't exist as long as people are happy."

In 1977, Filliou sent an enigmatic note to the Geneva-based gallery owner Marika Malacorda proposing a final development for his *Poussière de poussière* series: "A cardboard box / the stamp / the postcards, wrapped in a white cloth. Dust to dust from the… artistic effect."[77]

73   The boxes were produced in two different sizes. MAMCO owns 11 works of this series, bequeathed by Gérald Minkoff and Muriel Olesen or acquired thanks to the support of Karma Liess-Shakarchi and Rainer Michael Mason.

74   A widespread error in catalogs and monographs asserted that Filliou had dusted off works at MoMA in New York. The *Poussière de poussière de l'effet…* cloths exhibited at MAMCO and belonging to various other collections were exclusively used to clean works at the Louvre and the Musée National d'Art Moderne.

75   A "Boutique aberrante" stamp appears on some of the items in the series.

76   "Le coupe-ongles de Brancusi," in *Le Musée sentimental*, ephemera, May 1977. Our translations.

77   Malacorda Archives, consulted in May 2024. 1977 correspondence, undated handwritten note. Our translation.

OPTIMISTIC BOX NOS. 4 AND 5, ONE THING
I LEARNED SINCE I WAS BORN/THAT I MUST DIE
SINCE I WAS BORN

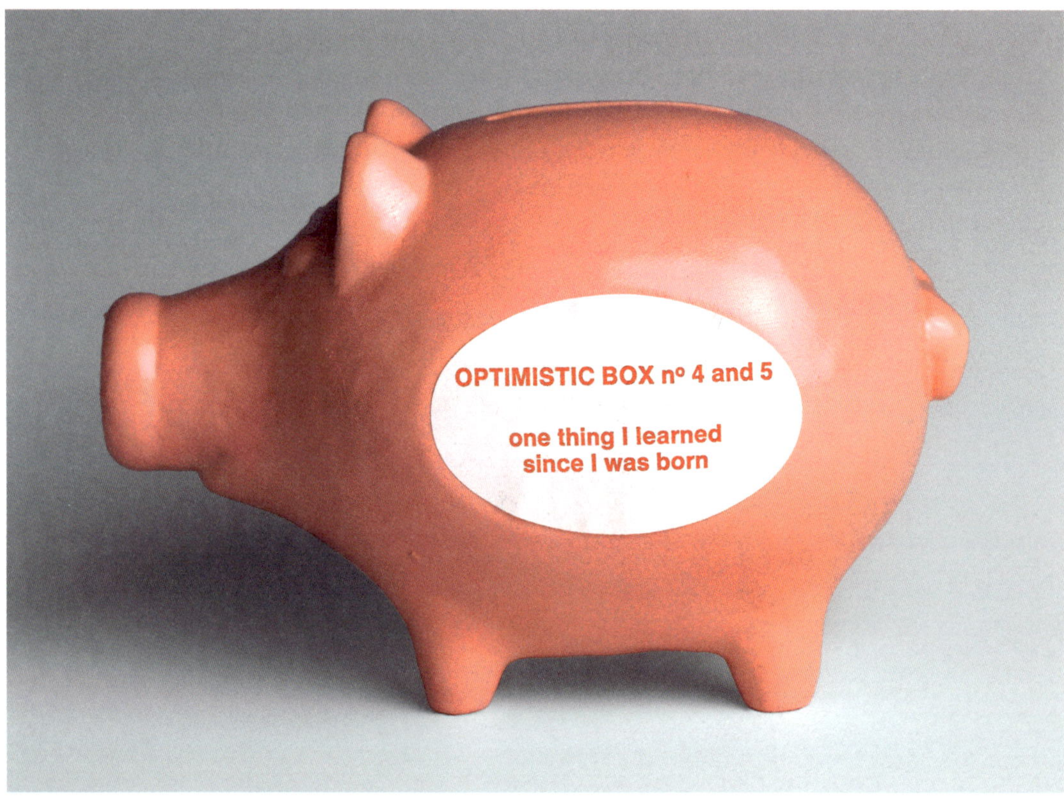

Optimistic Box Nos. 4 and 5, One thing I learned since I was born/that I must die since I was born, 1981 (based on a 1968 project)
painted piggy bank, plastic, printed paper
VICE-Versand, unlimited run
10.4 × 16 × 9.2 cm
MAMCO collection

Filliou and Wolfgang Feelisch originally planned to produce a series of five boxes, to be released by VICE-Versand under the generic title *Optimistic Boxes*. The first box was produced in 1968, and the second and third were made in 1969. However, it was not until 1981 that the final box in the series came into being. "All

                                                                                Robert Filliou

of them (No. 1, No. 2, No. 3 and No. 4/5) require viewers to read them in two stages (outside/inside or front/back)—a process that causes surprise, questioning or even awareness in the audience."[78]

> The first is a stone in a box. Outside, it reads: *thank God for modern weapons*, while inside, it reads: *we don't throw stones at each other anymore*. You already know the third one, don't you? It's about art. *So much the better if you don't know how to play chess: you won't imitate Marcel Duchamp*. The second concerns marriage: *Vive le mariage à trois*. The fourth should be shaped like a piggy bank with some money inside. This would be optimistic box No. 4, which says *it is great we are selfish*. And when you open it, it says: *we can keep our money for ourselves*. So we've been through war, love, art, money… And the last one can only be in English. It's a box in the shape of a small coffin, and on the lid, it says: *One thing I learned since I was born*. And inside, it says: *that I must die since I was born*. It's in English purely because of the double meaning of "since."[79]

When he combined boxes 4 and 5 in 1981, Filliou kept only the original wording, which he affixed to a piggy bank.

In the *catalogue raisonné* released by VICE-Versand, the publishing house's founder Peter Schmieder described Filliou's *Optimistic Boxes* "as a numbered series of individual works whose numbering is reminiscent of the Ten Commandments. The series should ultimately be understood as a succession of moralizing statements."[80] Yet Filliou was no preacher: his *Optimistic Boxes* were sufficiently ironic and ambiguous, in both their content and maxims, as to steer clear of moralizing territory. Rather, the artist wanted us to reflect on these statements—these "mind-openers"— on subjects that were important to him.

78   Sylvie Jouval, *op. cit.*, pp. 40–42 and 86–87. Our translation.

79   *Robert Filliou: The Secret of Permanent Creation*, *op. cit.*, p. 138. Our translation.

80   Peter Schmieder, *Unlimitiert: Der VICE-Versand Von Wolfgang Feelisch*, Buchhandlung Walther König, Cologne, 1998, p. 108. Our translation.

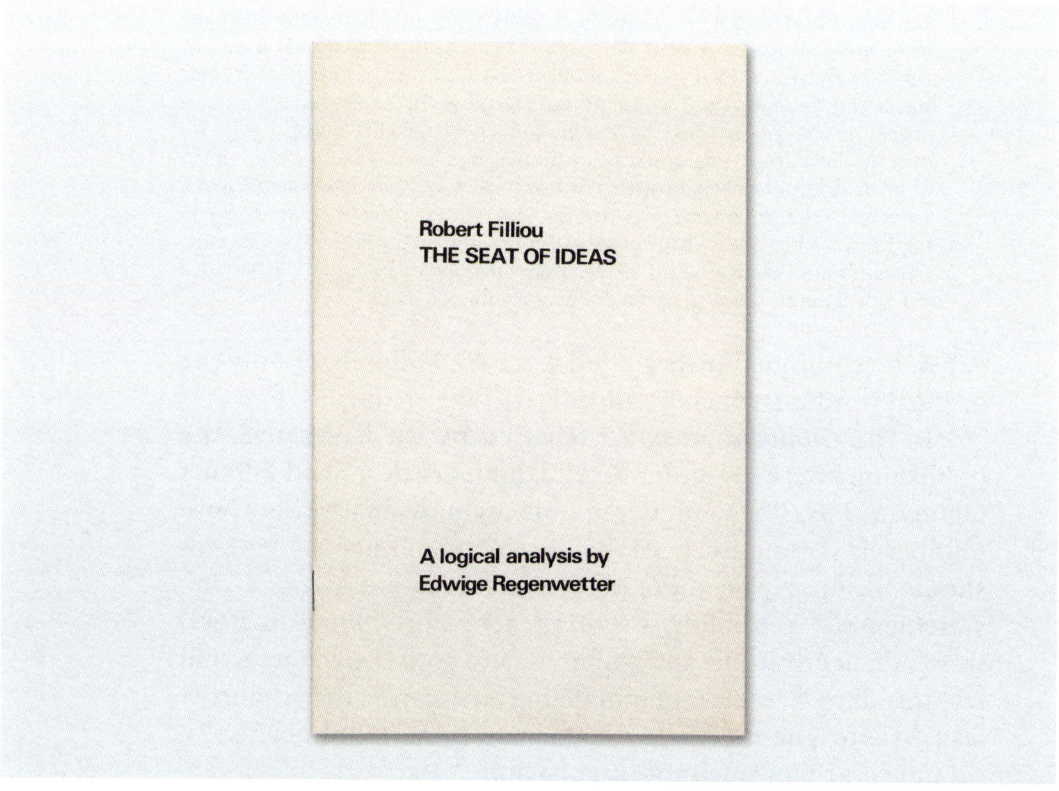

The Seat of Ideas: A logical analysis by Edwige Regenwetter, 1981
artist's book, softcover, bound, [32 p.], black-and-white illustrations, 13 × 21 cm
Syntax, Calgary, 900 copies
MAMCO collection, bequeathed by Gérald Minkoff and Muriel Olesen

This book, an English translation of *Le Siège des idées: Analyse logique de Edwige Regenwetter* published in 1977 by Lebeer-Hossmann, was produced in a limited run of 925 copies, including 25 deluxe copies bearing the inscription "*Sans voir et sans savoir*" (Without seeing and without knowing), written by Filliou in pastel. For this book, Filliou teamed up with Edwige Regenwetter, a friend and mathematics teacher at the Sorbonne. The former provided the seat and the latter supplied the logic.

Filliou had a longstanding interest in science, frequently conversing and collaborating with scientists so he could build his ideas on the latest research. In the book, Regenwetter constructs syllogisms and manufactures hypotheses with absurd conclusions:

> Does it destroy itself into an infinite number of empty parts, or does it vanish into an infinite number of infinitely small elements, ad infinitum? / If it destroys itself, it is because an infinite number of empty parts placed side by side cause it. It is a contradiction.[81]

The book had its origins in an earlier sculpture of the same name by Filliou, who was amused by the notion that a simple seat could serve as a platform for the expression of a thought or idea [FIG. 49]:

> The seat of ideas, dating from 1976, is the poorest object, the most destitute, the most devoid of aesthetic quality, as far removed from a work of talent as one can possibly imagine. It consists of the metal frame of a folding chair, to which a rectangular piece of cardboard is attached by a length of string to act as a backrest, bearing the words *LE SIÈGE DES IDÉES* (THE SEAT OF IDEAS) handwritten in capital letters. Nothing to sit on. It is an empty seat...[82]

81   *The Seat of Ideas...*, Syntax, Calgary, 1981, p. 17.

82   Pierre Tilman, *op. cit*, p. 231.

EINS. UN. ONE…

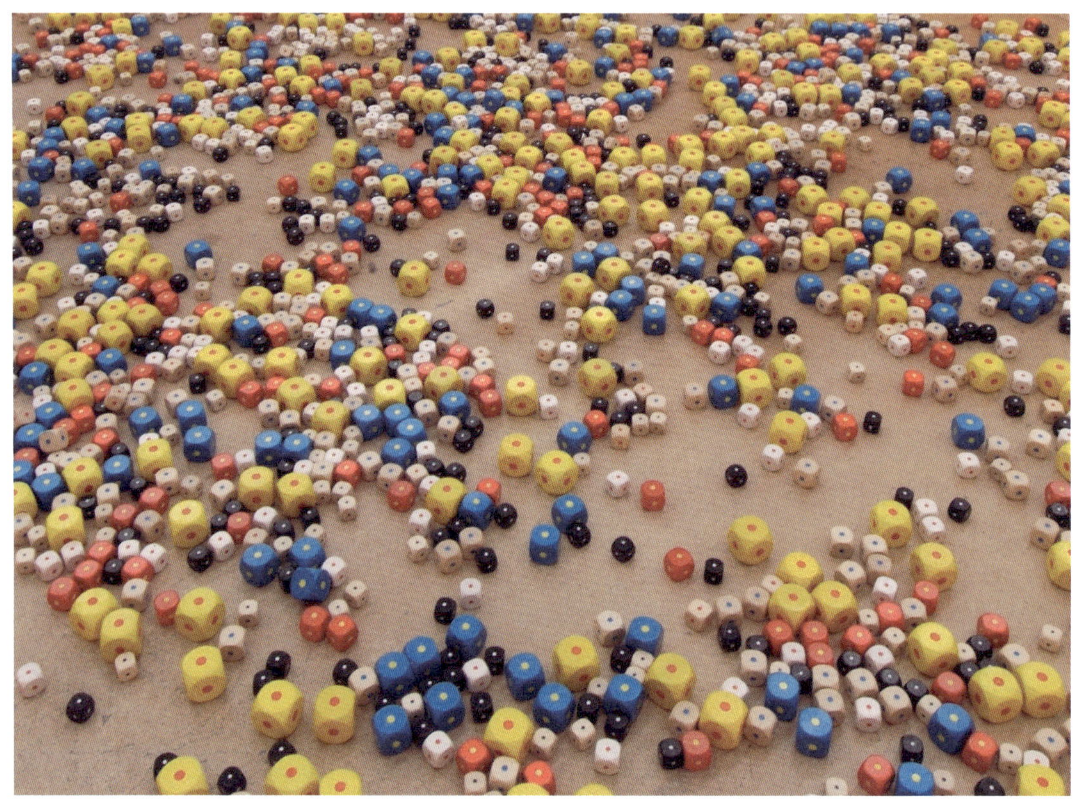

EINS. UN. ONE…, 1984
painted wood (dice of various colors and sizes)
circle with a diameter of between 6 and 9 meters
MAMCO collection

Filliou produced this work in 1984 after Kasper König invited him to participate in the exhibition *Von hier aus – Zwei Monate neue deutsche Kunst in Düsseldorf.* He had been an established part of the German art scene since the 1970s and, according to Wolfgang Feelisch, König considered him to be one of the most important representatives of 1960s art.

From a mundane, manufactured object—a die with only one dot on each face—Filliou created a singular work that was emblematic of his worldview. The sculpture itself is composed of a large number of dice (anywhere from 5,000 to over 10,000) of various sizes, in primary colors (red, yellow and blue), plus black, white and unpainted wood. The dots are in different colors: yellow, red or white, depending on the color of the die.

Once an instrument of choice for fortune-tellers, the die has become an integral part of many modern games. Blending play, creation and intuition ("the most powerful form of intelligence") was a common theme in Filliou's practice. He incorporated dice into several of his works, including *Valise Taoïste* (1961), a box containing two dice. Three faces of each die were marked with a "B" (for "*Bien*," or "Good") and the other three were marked with an "M" (for "*Mal*," or "Evil"). Throwing them opened up four possible combinations: BM (Good from Evil), BB (Good from Good), MB (Evil from Good) and MM (Evil from Evil).

EINS. UN. ONE… is a complex work in a simple form. The sculpture initially takes the form of a nine-meter-diameter circle enclosed by an 80-centimeter-high band of wood. The work is installed by throwing the dice onto the floor to create a unique, colorful constellation reminiscent of the mandalas[83] that symbolize the cosmos and the search for unity and fulfillment in Buddhist thought. The "holistic" nature of the work reflects the Buddhist view of life: being at one with the world. The first iteration of *EINS. UN. ONE…* was based on the "village structure" used in the exhibition *Von hier aus*, where each work had to be physically separated from the others. In the exhibition catalog, however, Filliou described two other ways the piece might be presented. The first was to spread the dice out in a spiral, a formal variant evoking the same cosmic interpretation as the circle. The second option was to give one die to each visitor, thus diluting and splintering the work into as many microcosms as there were carriers of the dice. As Filliou put it: "Art is not creating a painting, but causing a reaction through a painting." Art, which he preferred to call "Permanent Creation," had to contribute to our collective dream so that every human being could become a "happy loner"—just as the search for the essential structure of things was instrumental to living in the happy solitude of Fourier's phalanstery. For Filliou, it was not the now-obsolete center that mattered, but the "Eternal Network," as well as fun— a new and almost revolutionary form of energy.

Few other works in Filliou's oeuvre are as "monumental" as *EINS. UN. ONE…*: only pieces such as the *Poïpoïdrome* (a collaborative project with Joachim Pfeuffer), *Principle of Equivalence* and *Research on the Origin* can match it for scale. *EINS. UN. ONE…* was Filliou at his peak, his last great work. He retired to the Centre d'Etudes de Chanteloube in March 1985, stepping out of the public eye just as interest in his art was building to a crescendo. Filliou was the archetypal "Dharma Bum," a term coined by Jack Kerouac to describe the nomadic lifestyle of American bohemian writers and poets. He was a "man without qualities": he possessed a brilliant, intuitive mind, teased out the essential structure of things, used thought as a material and art as a unique source of energy and, like Fernando Pessoa, had in him "all the dreams of the world."

83   A drawing dated 1984 and belonging to Wolfgang Feelisch could have been an early sketch of *EINS. UN. ONE…*: it depicts a cross-shaped mandala in which dice are arranged in a mathematical pattern on a piece of yellow fabric. The drawing is reproduced in the Feelisch collection catalog: *Robert Filliou – Poet. Sammlung Feelisch*, exhibition catalog, Galerie der Stadt Remscheid, Remscheid, 1997, p. 99.

Imprint

Editorial Direction
  Lionel Bovier

Editorial Coordination
  Chloë Gouédard

Texts
  Michel Collet
  Sophie Costes

Cover
  EINS. UN. ONE..., 1984
  MAMCO Genève

Design
  Gavillet&Cie/Devaud

Types
  Apax, Practice (optimo.ch)

Production
  Musumeci S.p.A, Quart (Aoste)

Printed and bound in Europe

  Published by
  ARTBOOK|D.A.P.
  75 Brood Street
  Suite 630
  New York
  NY 10004
  www.artbook.com
  ISBN 978-2-940656-14-1

Photo Credits

Centre Pompidou, MNAM-CCI,
  Dist. Grand Palais RMM/Audrey
  Laurans: 68-69)
Centre Pompidou, MNAM-CCI,
  Dist. Grand Palais RMM/Georges
  Meguerditchian: 94
Centre Pompidou, MNAM-CCI,
  Dist. Grand Palais RMM/
  image Ville de Paris; photograph:
  Benjamin Katz: 104
Wolgang Feelisch: p. 3-11, 14-15
Fondation Bodmer, Genève;
  photograph Naomi Wenger: 42
Julien Gremaud: p. 31 (1, 3), 34 (4, 6, 7),
  48-49, 51, 53, 55, 61, 79 (15), 85, 96
Ilmari Kalkkinen: p. 12-13, 34 (5),
  37 (12), 98
Alice Malinge: 65
Annik Wetter: p. 31 (2), 36 (8, 9, 10),
  37 (11), 39, 45, 57, 63, 66, 70, 73, 75,
  79 (16), 82, 87, 89-91

The series "MAMCO Collection"
is realized thanks to the support
of the Leenaards Foundation.

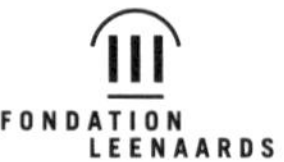

FONDATION
LEENAARDS

MAMCO
GENEVE

MAMCO Geneva
13, rue des Granges
CH–1204 Geneva
+41 22 320 61 22
info@mamco.ch

MAMCO opened in 1994 thanks to the perseverance of AMAM (Association for a Modern Art Museum, now Friends of MAMCO) and the generosity of eight patrons, who created the FONDATION MAMCO. Pooling together the support of its founders and, later, its co-founders, the foundation was the main source of funding and the sole governing body of the museum up until 2005, when it joined forces with the State and City of Geneva to create a public foundation, known as FONDAMCO.

MAMCO is overseen today by FONDAMCO, which is made up of FONDATION MAMCO, the Canton, and City of Geneva. FONDAMCO would like to thank all its partners, both public and private, and in particular: JTI, Fondation Leenaards, and Fondation VRM, as well as Fondation Bru, Fondation Coromandel, Fondation du Groupe Pictet, Fondation Lombard Odier, Lenz & Staehelin, Mirabaud & Cie SA, Christie's, and Sotheby's.

FONDAMCO

Philippe Bertherat,
  President
Ronald Asmar,
  Vice President
Anne Laure Bandle
Patrick Fuchs
Emmanuelle Maillard
Jérôme Massard
Carole Rigaut
Veronica Tracchia Lada Umstätter

FONDATION MAMCO

Council
  Philippe Bertherat,
    President
  Luis Freitas de Oliveira,
    Vice-President
  Jean Marc Annicchiarico,
    Treasurer
  Karma Liess-Shakarchi,
    Secretary
  Charles Beer
  Jean-Pierre Greff
  Emmanuelle Maillard
  Shelby du Pasquier
  Simon Studer

Founders
  Claude Barbey
  Jean-Paul Croisier
  Pierre Darier
  André L'Huillier
  Philippe and Jacqueline Nordmann
  Pierre Mirabaud
  Bernard Sabrier
  —as well as the Friends Association,
    represented by its President,
    Patrick Fuchs

Co-founders
  Anne-Shelton and Jean-Michel Aaron
  Antonie and Philippe Bertherat
  Marc Blondeau
  Maryse Bory
  Nicole Ghez de Castelnuovo
  Bénédict Hentsch
  Christina and Pierre de Labouchere
  Aimery Langlois-Meurinne
  Jean-Léonard de Meuron
  Nadine and Edmond de Rothschild
  Lily and Edmond Safra

Patrons
  Jean Marc Annicchiarico
  Antonie and Philippe Bertherat
  Association des Amis du MAMCO
  Verena and Rémy Best
  Marc Blondeau
  Bach-Nga Croisier
  Darier Family
  Angela and Luis Freitas de Oliveira
  Karma Liess-Shakarchi
  Emmanuelle Maillard
  Jean-Léonard de Meuron
  Pierre Mirabaud
  Shelby du Pasquier
  Marine and Claude Robert
  Bernard Sabrier
  Safra Foundation,
    represented by Samuel Elia
  Sophie Sallès de Meuron
  Simon Studer

TEAM

Lionel Bovier,
  Director

Museum Management
and Development
  Valérie Mallet,
    Administrator
  Damien Grimm,
    Development Manager
  Chloë Gouédard,
    Library, Archives,
    and Museum Resources
  Julien Gremaud,
    Digital Communication
  Viviane Reybier,
    Press and Communication

Exhibitions and Collection
  Julien Fronsacq,
    Chief Curator
  Françoise Ninghetto,
    Honorary Curator
  Elisabeth Jobin,
    Curator
  Charlotte Schaer,
    Collection Curator
  Cyrille Maillot,
    Chief Exhibition Productions
  Filipe Dos Santos,
    Exhibition Productions
    and Collection Registrar
  Benoît Charron,
    Transport Registrar
  Pierre-Antoine Héritier
  and Caroline Dick,
    Associate Restorers
  Annik Wetter,
    Associate Photographer

Public and Education Services
  Yann Abrecht,
    Public Services Manager
  Virginie Keller,
    Public Services Coordinator
  Franco Osses Vidal,
    Public Services Coordinator
  Charlotte Morel,
    Education Services Manager
  Julie Cudet,
    Education Services Coordinator

Facility Management and Surveillance
  Antonio Magalhaes,
    Chief of Facility Management
  Joana Gomes Da Silva,
    Facility Management

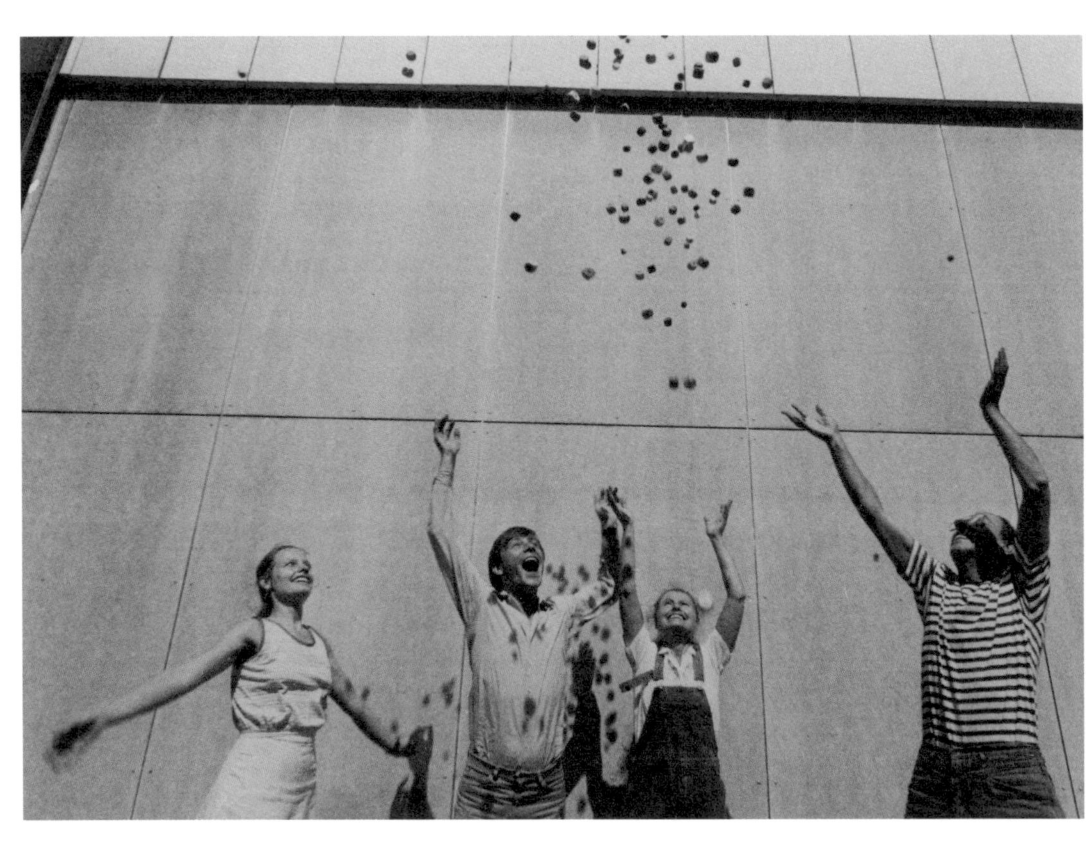